The Medieval Persian Gulf

T0327154

PAST IMPERFECT

Further Information and Publications
www.arc-humanities.org/our-series/pi

The Medieval
Persian Gulf

Brian Ulrich

British Library Cataloguing in Publication Data

A catalogue record for this book is available from the British Library.

© **2023, Arc Humanities Press, Leeds**

ISBN (print) 9781802700046
e-ISBN (PDF) 9781802701517
e-ISBN (EPUB) 9781802701524

www.arc-humanities.org

Printed and bound in the UK (by CPI Group [UK] Ltd), USA (by Bookmasters), and elsewhere using print-on-demand technology.

Contents

List of Illustrations

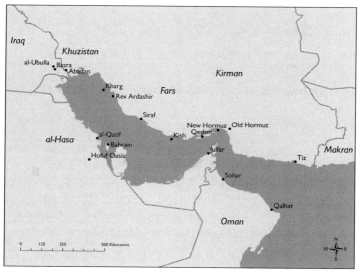

Map 1. The Persian Gulf, showing major places
mentioned in the text. Map by Jacob Hockenberry.
Used with permission.

Timeline

622	Muhammad's flight to Medina, beginning of Islamic calendar
632	Death of Muhammad
635–636	Traditional date for founding of Basra
656–661	First Civil War of Islam, involving the caliphate of ʿAli and including origins of Shurat
685–692	Second Civil War of Islam, when Muhammad is first mentioned in Muslim profession of faith and there were Shurat states in Khuzistan, Fars, and al-Hasa
700s	A general rise in prosperity leads to an increase in archaeological remains and the rise of the *tujjar* class; the Ibadis develop out of quietest Shurat in Basra
750	Beginning of Abbasid dynasty of caliphs
793–885	Stable Ibadi imamate in Oman
ca. 800	Building of Siraf's main mosque
800s	Clears signs of cultural islamization
ca. 830	Belitung shipwreck
869–883	Zanj Revolt led by ʿAli b. Muhammad
890s	Formation of Qarmatian state in al-Hasa
900s	Sunnism begins to spread in northern Oman
930s and 940s	Establishment of Buyid rule in Iran and Iraq
Late 900s	Earliest Shi'ite funerary inscriptions in Siraf
977	Earthquake devastates Siraf
1000s	Kish displaces Siraf

1040s and 1050s	Iran, Iraq, and Oman come under rule of Seljuqs, who develop greater trade infrastructure; ʿUyunids rise in al-Hasa and Bahrain
1051	Nasir-i Khusraw visits the Qarmatians and a diminished Basra
Early 1100s	Earliest evidence of Twelver Shiʿism on Bahrain; Banu Nabhan rise in Oman's interior
Late 1100s	Kish battles ʿUyunids for influence in Bahrain and al-Hasa; Benjamin of Tudela reports on the Gulf's Jewish communities
ca. 1200	Horses were regular part of Gulf trade by this time
1226	Beginning of the reign of Abu Bakr, under whom Salghurids rise in Gulf and defeat Kish, develop Bahrain
1250s	Mongol invasion of Iran and Iraq led by Hulegu
1260s–1306	Career of Jamal al-Din al-Tibi
1300	Baha al-Din Ayaz moves Hormuz's centre to Qeshm, and later Jarun
1329–1332	Ibn Battuta travels through the region
1332–1333	Qutb al-Din Tahamtan II makes Hormuz the Gulf's dominant power by defeating Kish
1335	Fall of the Ilkhanate
1400s	Height of Hormuz
1507–1515	Portuguese subjugate Hormuz

Introduction

In 2003, the American animation studio Dreamworks released as an intended summer blockbuster *Sinbad: Legend of the Seven Seas*. One movie preview described it as "fortuitously set in the Mediterranean," although the title character's name was that of *The Arabian Nights*' seafaring merchant who lived in Baghdad and set out on journeys from Basra. Although voice actor Brad Pitt was concerned that his Missouri accent was inappropriate for a Middle Eastern character, the filmmakers embraced it as a "mood lightener." Sinbad's heritage was thus obscured behind a story involving the Greek city-state of Syracuse on Sicily and Eris, Greek goddess of discord.[1]

It is no accident, however, that even in the contemporary United States the paradigmatic legendary seafarer would come from the Persian Gulf. It is, after all, the oldest body of water for which we have clear evidence of human sailing, as it connected the southern reaches of Mesopotamia with Bahrain, then known as Dilmun, which figured in myth as a paradise. Also connected by sea was Oman, a source of copper, and ultimately the valley of the Indus River in modern Pakistan, itself a land of great seafarers and important trading partners of the Gulf. Just as today over one third of the

---

1 "Sinbad: Legend of the Seven Seas (2003)," *EW.com*, April 25, 2003, https://web.archive.org/web/20120927152532/http://www.ew.com/ew/article/0,,444346,00.html.

world's crude oil passes through the Gulf, throughout ancient and medieval times the waterway was a crucial conduit for Indian Ocean luxury products.

The purpose of this book is to acquaint readers with the history of the Gulf as it relates to themes of cultural and religious diversity and that often hemispheric long-distance maritime trade which is the precursor to globalization. It will show that the Gulf has had people of diverse ethnic backgrounds since long before the age of oil, and that people adhering to different religious traditions have sometimes been in conflict in the region, but also easily coexisted, especially at the level of common believers. It will also show the importance of the region's long-distance trade to its culture and economy, as well as its significance for the Middle East more broadly.

Those whose image of Gulf history is focused on Bedouin and fisherfolk with small settlements along deserted coasts will, in fact, find those within. They will also, however, find Christian monks pursuing devotions in well-supported monasteries, enslaved people of African origin clearing agricultural land and harvesting crops, small-scale merchants with ambitions of becoming great traders, seafarers spinning yarns in cosmopolitan ports, and soldiers of fortune enlisted for defence and conquest. As a work of synthesis, this book will contain little that is new to specialists in the different topics touched upon. However, as the different time periods, research languages, and methods are too seldom considered as a whole, some new ideas may emerge from bringing them together.

Geography and Nomenclature

For the geographers and mariners of the Islamic Middle Ages, the Gulf was one of a string of seas connecting the Middle East ultimately with China. The earliest Arabic name we have for it is "Sea of Fars" (Persia), from an anonymous trader writing in 851, and that or similar names recur in the 900s. In these naming conventions, what mattered was not who controlled the sea, but rather the countries to which they distinctively led; the Gulf was the sea route to Persia as, in that time, on the Arabian coast, only minor ports lay between Iraq and the Strait of Hormuz. An anonymous Persian geography from the same period calls it the "Gulf of Iraq," while using "Arabian Gulf" for the Red Sea and "Persian Gulf" for the combination of the Gulf of Oman and Arabian Sea. The Portuguese also referred to the Gulf as "Persian Gulf" or "Persian Sea," and so the term passed into European usage. In the 1600s it increasingly came to be called the "Gulf of Basra," as that port to which it led was undergoing a renaissance, while the Gulf of Oman was often called "Gulf of Hormuz." By the 1800s, however, "Persian Gulf" was standard.[2]

Controversy over the Gulf's name began with twentieth-century nationalism and the idea of national domination of bodies of water and their shores. During the nineteenth century, the British became the Gulf's dominant power, and made treaty arrangements with the various Arab rulers along both its Iranian and Arabian Peninsula shores. Along the Iranian coast, these Arab rulers also recognized nominal Iranian sovereignty while maintaining their effective autonomy. After World War I, the Iranian government sought to drive out the British as a colonialist power and consolidate the central government's authority in its Gulf periphery. This included an awareness of geographical nomenclature. In 1933, an official in Khuzistan wrote to his superiors expressing concern over a local map which labelled the body of water the "Gulf of Basra" rather than the Persian Gulf.[3]

Iran's nationalists considered the Arabian coast from Kuwait to Muscat to be just as much theirs as the north shore and its associated islands, and the country did not renounce its claim to Bahrain until 1970. During the 1950s, Egypt began

---

2 C. Edmund Bosworth, "The Nomenclature of the Persian Gulf," *Iranian Studies* 30 (1997): 77–94.

3 This is a major theme of Chelsi Mueller, *The Origins of the Arab-Iranian Conflict: Nationalism and Sovereignty in the Gulf between the World Wars* (Cambridge: Cambridge University Press, 2020), with the account of the Khuzistan official on pages 88–89.

referring to the Gulf as the "Arabian Gulf" as part of its pro-
motion of pan-Arab nationalism in the region and in order to
counter Iran as a rival Middle Eastern power. Following the
1958 coup which brought an Arab nationalist government to
power in Iraq, the Iraqi government, too, began promoting the
name, hoping to gain influence among the Arabs who lived in
Khuzistan and along the shores of the Arabian Peninsula.

The choice of "Persian Gulf" in this book is driven simply by search engine optimization for the Anglophone world.
As is often the case in historical discussions of the Gulf, it
also includes the Gulf of Oman, also sometimes named after
the neighbouring Iranian region of Makran. This Gulf is separated from the Persian Gulf proper by the Musandam Peninsula and the Strait of Hormuz. The Musandam Peninsula is a
great rocky spur pointing towards Iran, one end of the Hajar
Mountain range which as one moves south into Oman forms
an arc twenty to thirty kilometres (twelve to eighteen miles)
from the sea, such that the actual coastline consists of the
Batina plain, sandy but with enough reserves of groundwater
to support settlements. Opposite this, Makran also features
mountains behind a coastal plain, but water on that plain is
much harder to come by, and so the denser settlement is
back in a "green belt" of mountain valleys.[4]

Most of Iran's Persian Gulf coast is also mountainous, with
only small, isolated spots for settlement and several noteworthy islands. The exception is Khuzistan, which along with
the neighbouring short coast of Iraq forms a marshy area
where the rivers of Mesopotamia and southwestern Iran dis-
charge into the sea. In this region the coastline has steadily
advanced even in the historic times covered by this book.
The Arabian coast, on the other hand, is mainly desert, with
a major oasis zone in eastern Saudi Arabia near the island
of Bahrain. "Bahrain" historically designated not only that
island, but also the broader eastern peninsula, though for the

---

4 The term "green belt" is from Fiorani Piacentini, *Beyond Ibn
Hawqal's Bahr al-Fārs*. (For short-form citations like this, see Further
Reading at the end, or an earlier citation above).

sake of clarity in this book we will refer to eastern Saudi Arabia by its more recent name of "al-Hasa."

The Indian Ocean does not have a year-round prevailing wind. Instead, at least in the northern hemisphere, strong winds called monsoons, related to the heating and cooling of Asia, blow predictably during certain seasons. From late April through August, monsoons blew from the southwest, and then reversed to blow from the northeast from November until into early March. Based on when the seas would be freer from storms, late April, May, and August were the best times to set out from the Gulf, and November and December to return to the Gulf from India. The voyage to India would have taken somewhat over a month, while the return to the Gulf somewhat less. If the ship sailed on to China, it would have to remain in India a time for conditions to be favourable, and then the same if it returned from China to the Middle East.

Historical Background

Islam began with the preaching of Muhammad in Mecca; the first year of the Islamic calendar is 622 CE, when he fled from Mecca to Medina and established in the latter the first community governed according to Islamic precepts. Muhammad's preaching was not that he was inaugurating a new religion, but rather that he was re-establishing a pure monotheism of Abraham that had been frequently revealed by God and yet corrupted by humans. After his death in 632, Islam was led for a generation by his associates, the "rightly guided caliphs," though it should be noted that the term is a Sunni one and Shi'ites believe that the fourth of those rightly guided caliphs, ʿAli, was the rightful leader all along. This was the period of the early conquests which led the caliphate to dominate the Middle East.

ʿAli's reign was taken up with the First Civil War, out of which emerged the rule of the Umayyad dynasty, with its capital in Damascus. Their attempt to establish a dynasty led to the Second Civil War from 685–692, when they asserted their claims while most regions of the newly conquered empire were led by people recognizing instead the son of a close companion of Muhammad who established himself in Mecca. The Umayyads prevailed, however, and continued to rule until 750 when they were displaced by the Abbasids, descendants of Muhammad's uncle ʿAbbas. This is the dynasty which established Baghdad as its capital soon after coming to power.

By the 900s, however, the Abbasids reigned more than ruled, and their actual power was usually eclipsed by other dynasties which conquered Baghdad and used them for legitimacy. The first of these was the Buyids, ethnic Daylamites from the mountains southwest of the Caspian Sea. Their heyday was the second half of the tenth century, though they lasted into the eleventh, when they were displaced by the Seljuq Turks, part of a general wave of Turkish migration from Central Asia into the Middle East. Finally, there were the Mongols. Although they became a Eurasian power under Chinggis Khan, who died in 1227, from the standpoint of Gulf history the invasion of the Middle East in the 1250s by his grandson Hulegu is more significant, as he both executed the last Abbasid caliph in Cairo and established the Ilkhanate, which ruled in Iran until 1335.

A word is in order about the many names one will encounter in this book. Arabic names historically indicated family relationships. Thus "Ibn," often abbreviated with just a "b" indicates "son of," while "ibna" or "bt" would be daughter of. When used alone, an "Ibn" compound will not always refer to the immediate parent, but instead sometimes feature a particularly prominent ancestor. "Umm" and "Abu" are not given names, but mean "mother" and "father," and are most commonly followed by the name of the firstborn son in an honorific added before the given name. These honorifics can, however, also be used metaphorically. As seen in the modern adjectives used for Arabian Peninsula countries, an "i" is associative, and thus "al-Sirafi" means "of Siraf." Finally, by the tenth century, prominent people would have an honorific added to their name. Called a *laqab*, this is a two-word phrase such as "Jamal al-Din," which means "Beauty of Religion," and either comes before a given name or is used independently. For names in other languages, it will be more convenient to address them as they appear.

Acknowledgements

I would like to thank Claire Hopkins for signing me to a contract when this book was still a half-formed idea in my mind, and Anna Henderson and the rest of the Arc Humanities staff who guided it through to completion. The press's anonymous reviewer, Christine Senecal, and Derek Kennet read the manuscript and made many useful comments. At Ezra Lehman Memorial Library, Nicole Kunkle and Jeff Milburn obtained for me a number of works necessary to write this book. Jacob Hockenberry made the book's map, and I would heartily recommend him for such work in the future. Finally, I would like to thank Simon Gallimore of Lingua Franca Television and Richard Mortel for their permission to reproduce photos.

Scholarship, of course, is a collective enterprise, and a book like this is made possible by many other people's painstaking research. The "Further Readings" at the end includes works of interest to those interested in exploring topics further, and several of these were also crucial sources for the present work. In order to keep citations to a minimum, works listed in Further Readings are rarely cited in the text, but in order to ensure people are properly credited for their insights and discoveries, other works do appear in footnotes. Finally, while this book does include the ʿ and ʾ for Arabic ʿayn and hamza, other diacritical marks from Arabic and Persian are omitted for simplicity in the main text.

Chapter 1

Religious Diversity of
the Early Islamic Era

In 2019, the municipal council of the island of Muharraq in Bahrain considered a petition to recognize a neighbourhood of a town called Dayr by its historic local name, an Arabic phrase meaning "Neighbourhood of the Monk." "Dayr" itself is the Arabic word for monastery, and together the two names recall flourishing Christian communities along the shores of the Persian Gulf, one centred around monasteries and individual holy men often believed to have miraculous powers. These Christians lived in a multi-religious Gulf too little known today, such that when in 2021 Jewish communities of the six Arab Gulf states established the Beth Din of Arabia as a new religious court for civil disputes over personal status issues, inheritance law, and kosher certification, news outlets called it the region's first communal organization, even though it might also have been cast as a rebirth of a once thriving Jewish religious life in the region.[1]

The existence of Christian, Jewish, and Zoroastrian communities in the medieval Persian Gulf is too often obscured

---

1 Mohammed Al ʿAli, "VIDEO: Bahraini Village with Christian Roots Draws Pilgrims," *GDN Online*, July 15, 2019, https://beta2. gdnonline.com/Details/569263/VIDEO-Village-with-Christian-roots-draws-pilgrims; Linda Gradstein, "Jewish Communities in Six Gulf States Announce Joint Association," *VOA*, https://www. voanews.com/a/middle-east_jewish-communities-6-Gulf-states-announce-joint-association/6202058.html.

even in scholarly overviews of the region's history, which still often focus on a narrative of Islam sweeping quickly across the peninsula and beyond, even though for other regions of the Middle East the fact that it was centuries before Islam became the majority religion has long been recognized. One problem has been that the most complete sources, those in Arabic, exist only from the 800s and later, while the Gulf sources from earlier times are more restricted in scope and often treated only by their own specialists. Taken together, however, they reveal a tapestry of people seeking their way amidst life's trials in a multi-confessional religious culture of both conflict and coexistence.

Religious Communities of the Sasanian Era

Prior to the rise of Islam, the dominant Persian Gulf power was the Sasanian Empire, which ruled Iran and Mesopotamia since the third century. The religion which formed the ideological basis of Sasanian rule was Zoroastrianism, though exactly what that consisted of during the period is uncertain, as our most systematic accounts are from ninth and tenth-century digests of Sasanian-era Zoroastrian texts. Called by its adherents simply the "Good Religion," Zoroastrianism was grounded in a collection of texts collectively called the Avesta, which refer to the teachings of an ancient figure named Zarathushtra, or Zoroaster to the Greeks. The world was divided into good and evil, but these were in a state of conflict and mixture awaiting the ultimate triumph of good over evil. Light was associated with good, and fire was a key element in the battle. For this reason, Zoroastrian rituals, performed by priests called magi, were performed in the presence of fire, and "fire-worshippers" would come to be an anti-Zoroastrian slur.

There were definitely Zoroastrians in the seventh-century Gulf region; however, information about them is scarce. Arabic sources refer to Zoroastrians in Oman and al-Hasa. More specifically, there are reports of adherence to Zoroastrianism among the tribe of Tamim, including by several prominent figures who mingled with the Sasanian nobility. Cemeteries in Rev Ardahsir, near modern Bushehr, include ossuaries with bones which had previously been exposed, a Zoroastrian practice to avoid contaminating the earth with decaying flesh. There are also possible Zoroastrian burials on Kharg, an island in the upper Gulf, and perhaps other islands near Iran's shores.[2]

The first major Christian populations in the Gulf may have been prisoners captured in the Sasanians' wars against the Roman Empire, prisoners who are reported as being settled in Khuzistan during the third and fourth centuries. Both Khuzistan and the region around Basra in what is now Iraq became important ecclesiastical sees during the 300s. Most of the eastern coast of Arabia was part of Beth Qatraye. This province was under the Bishop of Rev Ardashir, whose remit extended around the Indian Ocean. In 410, the Sasanian rulers organized their Christian subjects into the Church of the East, headed by the Patriarch of Seleucia–Ctesiphon, who took the additional title catholicos. Shortly thereafter, we also have the first record of a bishop from Beth Mazunaye, or Oman.

One sometimes sees the Church of the East described as Nestorian in its theology, but this is an accusation made by their rival Christians in other areas. Nestorius was a Patriarch of Constantinople who argued for a separation of the divine

---

2 Michael Lecker, "Tribes in Pre- and Early Islamic Arabia," 1–106 at 73–75, reprinted as item 11 (XI) in Lecker, *People, Tribes and Society in Arabia Around the Time of Muhammad*, Variorum Collected Studies (Aldershot: Ashgate, 2005); St. John Simpson, "Nomads and Monks, Soldiers and Sailors, Farmers and Fishermen: New Archaeological Insights into Life in the Persian Gulf from Late Antiquity to the Medieval Period," in *Ex Oriente Lux: Collected Papers to Mark the 75th Anniversary of Mikhail Borisovich Piotrovsky*, ed. A. A. Zolotva (St. Petersburg: State Hermitage Publishers, 2019), 288–335 at 293–94; E. Haernick, "Quelques monuments funéraires de l'île de Kharg dans le Golfe Persique," *Iranica Antiqua* 11 (1975): 144–67 at 164.

and human in Jesus. Arguing that the Virgin Mary should not be called "Mother of God," he insisted, "Mary did not give birth to a god. I cannot worship a god who was born, died, and was buried."[3] The Church of the East teaches rather that Jesus had two natures, one human and one divine, but still a single personhood, and thus a fusion of the divine and human. Even this doctrine only became firm orthodoxy during the 600s.

Apart from theologians and ecclesiastical leadership, simple Christian believers were usually far less attached to the doctrinal nuances of their confession than they were to the local institutions and holy figures who embodied divine power. When able to celebrate the liturgy, and among nomadic populations this might have been rare, they could absorb some doctrine. Important beliefs could also be set into hymns sung outside of church as work songs. More significant, however, was the belief in divine power, not only for salvation in the next life, but aid in this one. Life was filled with uncertainty, concerning illness and injury for oneself and loved ones, weather for crops and grazing land, occasional threats from violence, and any number of other things beyond the control of individuals. People shared stories of miracles, not only demonstrating the truth of one's confession through the mighty works of its champions, but the potential of holy men such as monks and hermits to mediate God's mercy with these everyday concerns. Most important of all was the power of the Eucharistic elements, the bread and wine which became the body and blood of Jesus, and which were not only taken in communion, but used as talismans against dangers both physical and spiritual.[4]

---

3 Karl-Heinz Uthemann, "History of Christology to the Seventh Century," in *Constantine to c. 600*, vol. 2 of *The Cambridge History of Christianity*, ed. Augustine Casaday and Frederick W. Norris (Cambridge: Cambridge University Press, 2007), 460–500 at 474.

4 A focus on "simple believers" and their religiosity is developed by Jack Tannous, *The Making of the Medieval Middle East: Religion, Society, and Simple Believers* (Princeton: Princeton University Press. 2018), with this material from 36–39, 63–67, 137–42.

We get a window into the world of the Church of the East in the Gulf via *The History of Mar Yawnan*, a hagiography which, although set in the 300s, was composed in the late 600s or early 700s and reflects that time period.[5] Much of the narrative is set in and around the Monastery of Mar Thomas on what is called the Black Island (see *Anthology of Syriac Writers from Qatar in the Seventh Century*, ed. Kozah et al., 3, 17). This could be one of several islands in the Gulf where archaeologists have discovered large early medieval monasteries. The largest of these, on Kharg, had not only a church and monks' cells, but a library, scriptorium, and education hall, highlighting the way monasteries were centres of formal learning as well as contemplation.

Mar Yawnan himself was not a monk, but rather an ascetic dedicated to solitary contemplation, who had earlier in his life been isolated in a reed hut for twenty years. He travelled to Mar Thomas in part to escape those who kept seeking his wisdom, but also to visit a local hermit, Abba Philon, who lived alone in a cave on another island several days away. Mar Thomas and his companion from the monastery, however, were able to miraculously reach it much more rapidly, partly by riding a giant crab which followed Abba Philon's commands. The holy men also exchanged blessed relics, as Abba Philon gifted Mar Yawnan a piece of his staff, while requesting a belt that had belonged to Mar Awgen (*Anthology*, ed. Kozah, 15–17, 27–30).

The Mar Yawnan account includes other miraculous occurrences, especially the healing miracles that were significant in the world of the simple believers. When one of the monks was staying in the house of a wealthy Omani merchant named Nuꜥaym, his son fell ill, whereupon the monk suggested he travel to the monastery to seek healing

---

5 Here I follow the dating and interpretation of the text and the economy of Gulf monasteries advanced by Richard Payne, "Monks, Dinars, and Date Palms: Hagiographical Production and the Expansion of Monastic Institutions in the Early Islamic Persian Gulf," *Arabian Archaeology and Epigraphy* 12 (2011): 91–111.

from Mar Yawnan. The boy died on the way, but was res-
urrected through the holy man's intervention. One of the
monks was healed of a swollen belly through drinking and
being anointed with water in which a cross had been rinsed.
Another man, a poor labourer with the Persian name Khusraw, fell and broke his thigh while gathering dates, which
Mar Yawnan bound and healed through prayer overnight.
Not all ailments were physical; Mar Yawnan divined that
the son of another man, Zarqon, was being tormented by a
demon because his father was keeping a concubine (*Anthology*, ed. Kozah, 20–25).

Island monasteries such as Mar Thomas were still acces-
sible by sea and clearly connected to the broader economy
of the Gulf. After his son was returned to life, the merchant
Nuʿaym donated the goods from a ship returned from China,
which the merchants sold for a substantial sum (*Anthology*, ed. Kozah, 22). Zarqon was "one of those who bring
up pearls from the ocean," and also made a substantial
donation (*Anthology*, ed. Kozah, 22–23). A monk from Mar
Yawnan's community in Iraq travelled to Beth Qatraye with
another pearl merchant from the region (*Anthology*, 32). The
donations from such patrons funded church improvements
and the purchase of agricultural lands, such as perhaps the
date orchard where Khusraw was injured. Wine was another
important commodity, important both for the Eucharist and
refreshment in an age before modern water purification when
alcohol in a beverage could guarantee it was safe to drink.

Nuʿaym's wife and Zarqon's concubine are the only
women mentioned individually in the text, though others
would be included as part of collective references to families
and households. Women, however, did have important roles
in the Church of the East. For example, as members of the
Daughters of the Covenant, parallel to a Sons of the Covenant, some women took vows of celibacy and simple living,
lived apart from the general community, and performed community service, such as in medical contexts, as well as liturgi-
cal singing. As noted above, hymns and liturgy were the main
ways of transmitting church doctrine, and so through their

choirs women played a role in passing on those teachings despite a ban on their formally instructing others.[6]

Finally, Judaism in the Persian Gulf region goes back to the Babylonian Exile, when with the destruction of Jerusalem in 586 BCE, many inhabitants of Judah were sent to the city of Babylon, around fifty miles south of modern Baghdad in central Iraq. There many of their descendants remained even after a decree of the Achaemenid Persian ruler Cyrus the Great allowed them to return and rebuild the temple. In the early centuries of the common era, many in lower Iraq converted to Judaism, as seen archaeologically by the replacement of pagan temples with synagogues. It was likely during this period that they also spread in appreciable numbers into southern Iraq, and ultimately beyond, as there are reports of Jews in eastern Arabia during the time of Muhammad. Arabic sources also mention Jews along the coasts of al-Hasa, while there are Jewish graves on Kharg.[7]

Islam

The challenge for writing the early history of Islam is that the most complete and influential sources come from long after the period of Muhammad's life and the earliest conquests. These sources are the accounts of Muslim historians writing in Arabic, which we have in texts from the 800s and later. These texts do preserve older material, probably as old as at least the turn of the eighth century, but that is still several decades after Muhammad's death in 632. For our purposes, one problem is that while, like all religions, Islam developed over a significant period, these accounts present it as being mostly formed in Muhammad's lifetime. In addition, these

---

6 Susan Ashbrook Harvey, "Women and Children in Syriac Christianity: Sounding Voices," in *The Syriac World*, ed. Daniel King (London: Routledge, 2018), 554–59.

7 Michael Morony, *Iraq after the Muslim Conquest* (Princeton: Princeton University Press, 1984), 306–7; Haernick, "Quelques monuments funéraires," 165.

accounts, often written by people connected to the caliphal courts, served to legitimize the Islamic empire which was then at its height by presenting the caliphs as heirs of far-sighted and righteous predecessors who had managed divinely supported conquests.

Despite this, we can offer a basic outline narrative. Islam arose in western Arabia in the early seventh century through the preaching of Muhammad, a merchant from the city of Mecca. Through him God sent revelations which, after his death, were collected into the Qur'an, which Muslims regard as God's direct speech. During his life, Muhammad experienced persecution as his community grew, and in 622 he fled from Mecca to accept a position of authority in Medina, an event which later Muslims used as the start of their calendar. Military conflict ensued between Mecca and Medina, and Muhammad ultimately returned victoriously to Mecca, where the population embraced Islam. According to the medieval Muslim accounts, most of Arabia accepted Muhammad's preaching shortly thereafter, though this is debated in modern scholarship.

Historians can reconstruct the earliest layer of Muslim belief in part by examining the Qur'an and inscriptions from the first generations of Muslims. Although later exegetes would read other references into the text, taken by itself, the Qur'an mentions only four seventh-century personages by name, five roughly contemporary events, and a handful of places and tribes or peoples. However, it does shed light on the values and attitudes of those who took it as divine. Perhaps the most prominent theme, especially in the Qur'an's earliest sections, is the imminence of judgment by the one true God, but also the possibility of divine mercy in that judgment. This matches the emphasis of those identifiably Muslim inscriptions from the religion's first decades, which emphasize God, his mercy, and a petitioner's need for forgiveness.[8]

---

8 For the count of historical references in the Qur'an see Sean Anthony, *Muhammad and the Empires of Faith: The Making of the Prophet of Islam* (Oakland: University of California Press, 2020),

The Qur'an emphasizes how God had continually sought to guide humanity through revelation to prophets, and stories of these prophets are a vehicle for emphasizing the importance of faith. In this way the Qur'an includes its own version of the sacred histories of Judaism and Christianity. The individual most named in the Qur'an is Musa, Arabic for "Moses," and the accounts of his life closely parallel those of the Torah. The main narrative account is in the 28th surah, or chapter, and here we can also see how the Qur'an emphasizes moral lessons. The value of repentance, for example, is shown when Musa begs God's forgiveness for killing an Egyptian, while the proud pharaoh and his army are destroyed in the sea, and all this is set up as a direct warning to the pagans of Mecca. ʿIssa, or Jesus, also appears in the Qur'an, and accounts of him include stories similar to some from non-canonical gospels, such as speaking from his cradle to defend his mother from accusations of fornication when she gave birth to him unwed. A clear line is also drawn between Muhammad's revelation and standard forms of Christianity, in that Jesus is simply a prophet and the idea of divine sonship is explicitly rejected.

The core of piety in the Qur'an is prayer, and establishing regular communal prayers is inevitably listed in the text as a key element of a group becoming Muslim. Also significant is freely given charity, and Qur'an 2:177 lists its uses as aiding relatives, orphans, travellers, other seekers of aid, as well as paying to free the enslaved. This charity was separate from *zakat*, which was paid to Muslim authorities based on one's wealth so as to purify what was retained, similar to tithing in Judaism and Christianity. The earliest term for Muhammad's followers was not "Muslims," but rather "Believers." The latter occurs many times more in the Qur'an than does "Islam" or "Muslim," and inscriptions make clear that the ear-

---

12–13, while the epigraphic record is compiled in Ilkka Lindstedt, "Who Is In, Who Is Out? Early Muslim Identity through Epigraphy and Theory," *Jerusalem Studies in Arabic and Islam* 46 (2019), 147–246 at 162–64.

liest leaders of the community after Muhammad had the title "Commander of the Believers." Finally, the Muslim profession of faith at this stage was simply "There is no God but God."[9]

By the ninth century, Muslim historians had divided the expansion of the Islamic state in the decades following Muhammad's death into two stages. To understand the first stage, the Wars of the Ridda, we need to remember that the later Arabic historians presented the Arabian Peninsula as having wholly adopted Islam during Muhammad's life. After his death, however, many chose to follow new prophets who had arisen, and the Muslim leadership in Medina waged war for two years to regain their loyalty; "ridda" is Arabic for "apostasy." Thereafter began the second stage, the conquest of the entirety of the Sasanian Empire and the Byzantine Empire south of modern Turkey.

The reality was not so neat. From 602 to 628, the Byzantines and Sasanians were involved in a major war which shook both empires to their foundations, and when the Byzantines finally won, the Sasanians were thrown into turmoil. After that happened, eastern Arabian leaders who had been Sasanian dependents turned to Muhammad's polity to secure their authority. When Muhammad died, such leaders did not automatically retain their loyalty to his successors, and, for example, rejected their tax collectors. At the same time, for some decades, tribes from the Arabian Peninsula had been expanding beyond it, driven by the search for pastures. Only over decades did the Muslim central authorities establish control over populations around the Gulf. The broader narratives of ridda wars and conquests arose for ideological reasons later, and local accounts which were often not well-anchored chronologically in people's memories were fitted into them.[10]

---

9 The early use of the term "Believers" comes from Fred M. Donner, *Muhammad and the Believers: At the Origins of Islam* (Cambridge, MA: Belknap, 2010), 57–58, 98–99, 112. The book also includes a reconstruction of Qur'anic piety.

10 For a defence of this model, see Brian Ulrich, *Arabs in the Early*

A crucial development from the perspective of Gulf history was the foundation of the city of Basra in the 630s. As the Islamic state expanded, it established garrison cities to settle nomads, administer the population, and keep a military force in strategic locations. Basra, at the head of the Gulf just inland from the port of al-Ubulla, was one of these, and particularly settled by tribes from the banks of the Euphrates all the way down to Oman. Initially a set of tribal encampments around a pre-Islamic market, upon becoming a garrison city Basra also acquired government buildings. Over the early Islamic centuries it became known for its many canals, and even today it is called "the Venice of the Middle East."

It was in the wake of the Second Civil War mentioned in the introduction that Islam developed more of its now familiar identity and ritual. For example, from the 690s on, "and Muhammad is the messenger of God" was added to the profession of faith, and "Islam" and "Muslim" were increasingly used to describe the new religion and its adherents. More detail of ritual is also spelled out. Whereas the Qur'an's statements about prayer are often vague, the Umayyad period saw a standardization of the five prayer times per day with their particular words and prostrations. People also turned to hadiths, accounts of Muhammad's words and deeds, to supplement the Qur'an. Gradually, over the course of the 700s and 800s, an Islamic jurisprudence arose based on the Qur'an and hadith corpus.

Religion in the Early Islamic Gulf

The Christian monastic communities of the Gulf continued to materially prosper during the first two centuries of Muslim rule. As will be discussed in chapter three, the rise of the caliphate brought an economic boom to the Gulf, and Christian communities participated, increasing the resources

Islamic Empire: Exploring al-Azd Tribal Identity (Edinburgh: Edinburgh University Press, 2019), 68–69.

that could flow into monasteries. In addition, many Muslims respected monks for their ascetic lifestyle, and there is evidence that monks and hermits were protected by order of Muslim leaders. We have a corpus of letters from Ishoyahb III, catholicos of the Church of the East from 649 until 659, in which he states that Muslims aided churches and monasteries.

The elimination of the Sasanian state also created an opening for church leaders to more firmly establish their authority over their flocks in matters previously influenced by imperial law. For example, Bishop Shemʿon of Rev Ardashir wrote a treatise on inheritance. More significantly, a church council held on Tarut Island near al-Qatif in al-Hasa promulgated a number of canons to regulate church life, such as bringing marriage entirely under the supervision of the clergy. From then on, the church would only recognize marriages properly blessed by a priest, and disputes regarding marriage were to be heard in ecclesiastical courts. Couples who married outside the church would be barred from the Eucharist.[11]

The Gulf was not a backwater for Christians, and during the early Islamic centuries gave rise to several writers who became known far beyond its shores. The most famous was Isaac of Nineveh, a Beth Qatraye monk who in the seventh century became bishop of Nineveh for a time before taking up a solitary life in Khuzistan. His theological works are still read today. He also had a brother, Gabriel Qatraye, who was known as "Interpreter of the Church." Another monk of Beth Qatraye, Dadisho, wrote works on the ascetic life that were known centuries later and as far away as Central Asia. During the mid-800s, Ishodnah, Bishop of Basra, wrote a now lost history, as well as other works, including a poem about Mar Yawnan which survives today.

---

11 Lev Weitz, *Between Christ and Caliph: Law Marriage, and Christian Community in Early Islam* (Philadelphia: University of Pennsylvania Press, 2018), 46, 53–55.

Scholars understand little about the process and rate of conversion to Islam in the early Islamic Gulf. The political conversions of east Arabian leaders may have represented simply political loyalty with little shift in practice or belief. As noted earlier, many of Islam's distinctive theological doctrines and practices took time to develop, and especially among simple believers, the boundaries among religious groups could often be uncertain. When the Muslim profession of faith was simply "There is no God but God," other monotheists could endorse it without scruples. Even during the 700s, there were Jews and Christians willing to accept Muhammad as a prophet specifically to the Arabs, and some Muslim groups were willing to consider such people converts.

In the same letter to Rev Ardashir which mentions the Muslim support for monks and priests, Ishoyahb III also refers to a mass conversion to Islam in Oman. As recounted by Ishoyahb, no violence was involved, and remaining a Christian would only have meant paying a portion of their property. He saw this as a result of a schism in which Shemʿon of Rev Ardashir was asserting his independence from the catholicos, followed by most of the Gulf bishops under him. From Ishoyahb's perspective, this alienation from the true church meant that the sacraments and other miraculous powers were ineffectual.[12] Multiple Omani figures are noted as former Christians in the Arabic sources, such as one from Dibba who later became the first Muslim judge in Basra.

The accounts of a man named al-Khirrit b. Rashid al-Naji show the shifts in religion that could happen in this period and how religion crossed with other forms of identity. Al-Khirrit was a Bedouin follower of ʿAli, mentioned in the introduction as the one whom Shi'ites believe was the rightful leader of Islam. During the First Civil War, al-Khirrit chose to renounce his loyalty and await a consensus leader for the Muslim community. He passed through Basra and into Khu-

---

12 This interpretation of Ishoyahb's letters is from Iskandar Bcheiry, *An Early Christian Reaction to Islam: Išūʿyahb III and the Muslim Arabs* (Piscataway: Gorgias, 2019), 128–33, 141–49.

zistan with a band of several hundred followers drawn from his tribe and non-Muslims seeking to avoid taxes, but was defeated en route to a fortress in the hills of Khuzistan by an army sent by ʿAli. From there, he fled to Oman, rallying his own tribe in particular and even killing ʿAli's governor. His followers in that country included both Christians and Muslims; the tribal solidarity outweighed the religious. Notably, there were also Christians who had converted to Islam and then reverted, though when al-Khirrit's army was defeated, they became Muslims once more. The Christians were taken prisoner and sent to Khuzistan, where they were ransomed by ʿAli's governor due to tribal ties.[13]

Zoroastrianism also continued in the Gulf for centuries after the rise of Islam. Merchants of that religion were prominent in the major port cities of Siraf and Sohar, and there are reports of them paying the poll tax in al-Hasa. About conversion to Islam, however, we again know little. Some Sasanian military units joined the Muslims in Basra, and this is presented as conversion by the later Arabic sources. There is also an interesting possibility in the archaeology of the hinterland of Rev Ardashir. There, a settlement near the modern village of Deh Qaʿed declined at the same time that the medieval Islamic city Tawwaj developed around ten kilometres (six miles) away. Similar shifts elsewhere may have resulted from Zoroastrians ostracizing converts to Islam, who then formed their own communities. This, however, remains speculative.[14]

---

13 The primary sources for these events are cited in Wilkinson, *Ibâḍism*, 145–46. They disagree on the geography of al-Khirrīt's flight after Khuzistan and the final battle, but the edge of Oman makes the most sense.

14 R. A. Carter, K. Challis, S. M. N. Priestman, and H. Tofighian, "The Bushehr Hinterland Results of the First Season of the Iranian–British Archaeological Survey of Bushehr Province, November–December 2004," *Iran* 44 (2006): 63–103 at 97–98; Jamsheed Choksy, *Conflict and Cooperation: Zoroastrian Subalterns and Muslim Elites in Medieval Iranian Society* (New York: Columbia University Press, 1997), 87.

The ongoing significance of the Jewish community in Iraq is seen in the fact that, from 676 until 688, coins with Hebrew letters were struck in Basra. That city was home to a religiously vibrant community some members of which kept company among the caliphate's elite. In the seventh century, one learned man left his whole fortune to the support of religious learning. The first Jew to write in Arabic was said to be a physician during late Umayyad times who translated works from Aramaic while also writing his own. Around 800, one man was part of a family who reportedly knew the entire Torah by heart. He was active in translating Persian works into Arabic; a contemporary of his translated the Torah and gospels. Another Jew actively engaged in religious disputation with Muslims.[15]

Although many believers could be drawn to sources of holy power and charisma regardless of their actual religion, religious authorities did try to draw firm boundaries. Zoroastrian magi, for example, often objected to Muslim, Christian, and Jewish burial practices which they saw as polluting the earth. Muslim leaders sought to segregate converts and assess the taxes on non-Muslims. The 676 Church of the East synod contained stipulations against contributing oil or candles to non-Christian houses of worship, and particularly sought to prevent social interactions between Christians and Jews. Such regulations, however, merely testify to the types of cross-religious interactions that were happening.

Kharijites and Ibadis

The first sectarian movement in Islam arose amidst the dispute over leadership in Islam (or the Believers' movement) between Muʿawiya, who would found the Umayyad dynasty, and ʿAli. When the latter agreed to submit to human arbitration during the First Civil War, some of his followers deserted,

---

15 Moshe Gil, *Jews in Islamic Countries in the Middle Ages* (Leiden: Brill 2004), 279, 282, 296–98.

associating themselves with the slogan "Judgment belongs to God alone." For this reason, they are called "Kharijites," which comes from an Arabic word meaning "to depart." Rather than this usually derogatory term, however, Kharijites referred to themselves as the "Shurat" (sing. *shari*), or "Exchangers." This referred to their willingness to exchange their life for the next through dying in battle on behalf of what they saw as righteousness, or, if not that, at least exchanging the everyday world for a more ascetic lifestyle (Gaiser, 47–51).[16] Such ascetic practices included long hours in worship, night vigils, tonsure, and at times even celibacy (Gaiser, 72–74). Ibadism, which is today still a branch of Islam prominent in Oman, emerged out of the Shurat.

In keeping with the Late Antique period's identification of religious groups with holy figures, the Shurat grounded their identity in part through particular martyrs whom they commemorated in poetry. Their first martyrs were those killed in battle in 658 at a place called Nahrawan, where ʿAli's army defeated them after they had killed some Muslims for not agreeing with their views. Three years later, one of them assassinated ʿAli. The 660s and 670s in southern Iraq were marked by occasional small Shurat uprisings against Umayyad governors, generally involving only a few dozen people. The best remembered was that of Abu Bilal Mirdas b. Udayya who was moved to revolt when the Umayyad governor in Basra executed an elderly woman who frequently criticized him. Together with thirty companions he fled Basra and, attracting additional companions along the way, fled to Khuzistan and eventually to Fars, where he and his band were killed in 681 (Gaiser, 48–66).

Today in Muslim theological circles, groups such as al-Qaeda and the Islamic State of Iraq and Syria are often called modern Kharijites because they encourage withdraw-

---

16 This discussion of the early Shurat is drawn from Adam Gaiser, *Shurāt Legends, Ibāḍī Identities: Martydom, Asceticism, and the Making of an Early Islamic Community* (Columbia: University of South Carolina Press, 2016), with specific pages cited in parentheses.

ing from society to what they see as a pure Islamic community, openness to martyrdom, and declaring that Muslims who disagree with them are effectively non-Muslims and liable to be fought. This last characteristic, however, was not true of all early Shurat. In an address to his followers, Abu Bilal, who was among the most respected figures by later Shurat, advocated departure from Basra as a way to ensure that they would fight only those who deliberately chose to stand against them as they sought to combat what evils they could (Gaiser, 65).

One group which did anathemize and fight other Muslims was the Azraqites, named for their first leader, Nafi'a b. al-Azraq. They emerged in the vicinity of Basra during the Second Civil War and threatened to take the city before being driven to Khuzistan. To the Azraqites, even children were reportedly to be killed or taken prisoner if they were not from a family that agreed with Azraqite beliefs and acted upon them in the expected ways, though in practice there seems to have been some occasional ambiguity on these points. Although they were able to establish a state capable of minting coins, during a grinding war during the 690s in which the Umayyad forces were led by a commander named al-Muhallab b. Abi Sufra, they were eventually driven out to Fars and further east in Iran before their defeat at the end of the decade. Adherents to their doctrines may have survived into later times, however (Gaiser, 68–70, 103–4, 106–11).

Another Shurat group, the Najdites, disagreed with the Azraqites on the points of attacking quietists, women, and children. They emerged in the large oasis which contains modern Riyadh, and are named after their leader Najda b. 'Amir al-Hanafi and not the region of Najd in central Saudi Arabia. Beginning with the conquest of eastern Saudi Arabia, they came to control much of the Arabian Peninsula by 687, but then fell into dissension. Najda was assassinated by his former followers in 691, and his successor, holding out in the old market town of al-Musha'qqar, was defeated and killed sometime thereafter. The group persisted, however; a Najdite leader again ruled in eastern Arabia from 724 until 732, and there were still reported adherents into the 800s.

Ibadism developed out of quietist Shurat during the 700s in Basra and later Oman and North Africa. In particular, it developed among those taught by a man named Jabir b. Zayd, who died in Basra during the first quarter of the eighth century. Among those who looked to him as an authority were several women from the family of the general al-Muhallab, as well as one of his sons who was commander of the Umayyad security forces in lower Iraq. This family had a base of power and tribal ties in Oman, and other Omanis who had settled in Basra were also among Jabir's followers. More broadly, due to developments beyond the scope of this book, by the mid-700s, those with ties to southern Arabia were particularly likely to oppose the Umayyads (Gaiser, 115–17).[17]

This led to the first Ibadi attempts to establish their own domains outside the control of the Umayyads and Abbasids. In the 740s, an Ibadi state arose in the highlands of Yemen, and it quickly took over Mecca and Medina, only to be just as quickly defeated. Notably, many in Basra also pledged loyalty to its imam, who called himself "Talib al-Haqq," or "Seeker of Truth." Immediately upon its fall, Ibadis in Oman proclaimed as their imam al-Julanda b. Masʿud, a descendant of the family which had ruled the country at the dawn of Islam and still remained prominent. Only with great difficulty did the new Abbasid dynasty suppress it in a vicious battle. The exact dates are uncertain, but the state lasted for only two years.

In 793, however, after a period in which the Abbasids ruled Oman, often through members of the same al-Julanda family, the Ibadis established a new imamate. In line with Shurat principles, the leader was chosen by a council of religious leaders with which he was expected to rule in consultation. Although religiously known as the imam, the state leader also took the old title of "Commander of the Believers." The idea of the Shurat evolved into a sort of volunteer military force which practised tonsure and celibacy alongside a willingness

---

17 On the extent of Jābir's Omani following, see Wilkinson, *Ibâḍism*, 188–89, 197.

to die in divine causes, though whether this was ever the case in practice is uncertain. This new Ibadi imamate, however, would last as a significant Gulf power for a century (Gaiser, 117–50).

* * *

As with other religions, Islam underwent a period of development as the earliest generations of Muslims worked out the meaning of their religion, developing different interpretations as they did so. At the same time, the Christian, Jewish, and Zoroastrians communities continued to prosper, and simple believers sought aid in life's struggles from many different sources of sacred power. As we will see in the next chapter, this religious diversity was matched by a diversity of languages and ethnicities.

Chapter 2

Ethnic Diversity

As described in the introduction, today the name of the Gulf, either Persian or Arabian, is a matter of international dispute linked to historic claims and recent ambitions. Along with this goes also the rise of nationalism, nationalism based on a concept of nation-states as usually ethnically homogenous. In the Gulf, this means that Iran has sought to Persianize its Gulf regions as effectively as possible, while the Arab states routinely present through their heritage industry a purely Arab and sometimes even Bedouin past while worrying about the presence of large numbers of guest workers, particularly from South Asia, as threats to that heritage.

The ethnic composition of the Gulf, however, has long been diverse. Language is not a sure guide to ethnicity, but from the early medieval period up until today, speakers of Arabic and Persian have lived mingled together all around its shores; hymns in Beth Qatraye were sung in Persian, even as most people's vernacular was close to Arabic. Significant populations of South Asian origin also stretched along at least the upper Gulf in Late Antiquity, forming a recognizable element with a remembered association with the subcontinent, but over the generations becoming part of the regional fabric steadily augmented by both voluntary migration and slavery. People from different regions of sub-Saharan Africa were also brought as slaves to the region down the centuries, and they, too, became a recognizable group even into the present.

Arabs and Persians

"Arab" was at first an ancient Mesopotamian term for those living in the desert between Mesopotamia and the fertile lands along the Mediterranean. Later, "Arabia" became the name of a Roman province stretching from the Sinai Peninsula into what is now Jordan, and inhabitants of this province called themselves "Arabs."[1] In the following centuries, however, the identity seems to have become much vaguer and far less commonly invoked, perhaps the way "North American" might apply to inhabitants of the continent but has little practical significance. In poetry written in Arabic by north Arabians before the seventh century, the broadest identity is generally Maʿadd. This term referred to the largely autonomous peoples living south of the heartlands of the Ghassanids in what is now Jordan and the Lakhmids by the Euphrates, two Arabic-speaking client dynasties of the Byzantines and Sasanians respectively.[2]

During the seventh century, however, ideas of Arab ethnicity grew in importance. Garrison cities such as Basra became home to people from very different regions in Arabia with their own lifestyles, political formations, and cultural observances, though having a common new religion and dialects which were usually mutually intelligible. Their new position as a privileged class led them to articulate commonality based on the idea of Arabness, a quality not shared by those over whom they ruled (Webb, 126–32). What that meant, however, was continually contested. For example, the Arabic words for "Arab" and "Bedouin" are similar, though whether they are etymologically related is uncertain (Webb, 319–21). A poet from what is now Kuwait who was settled in Basra attacked the al-Azd of Oman as not truly Arab, alleging they lacked

---

1 Robert Hoyland, "Reflections on the Identity of the Arabian Conquerors," al-ʿUṣūr al-Wusṭā 25 (2017): 113–40 at 127–30.

2 Peter Webb, *Imagining the Arabs: Arab Identity and the Rise of Islam* (Edinburgh: Edinburgh University Press, 2016), 70–85. References to this book in the following paragraphs are in parentheses.

nomadic heritage, were more familiar with ships than horses, and had physical features which were like those of settled peoples, and such attacks on them persisted for centuries.

One common view held that the Arabs were all those with Arab genealogies. We can see the importance of genealogy to Arabian life in the naming system described in the introduction, and for many in Arabia it structured everyday life by indicating connections which both imposed mutual obligations and allowed for access to collective resources. In Arabia, such networks included ties formed through women, such as through marriages and maternal relations. During the early Islamic period, however, elite men in the garrison cities and perhaps elsewhere often married women from conquered populations or took them as concubines, and such women came to be cut out of genealogy for the purposes of identity, which became strictly patrilineal as a means of claiming pure Arabness (Webb, 197–204).

Separated from the practical world of close kinship relations, however, there was a usually more abstract world of relationships among large groups, analogous to the way the twelve tribes of the ancient Hebrews were said to be descended from the sons of the Biblical Jacob. It was at this level that groups were incorporated into Arabness, as prominent figures in early Islamic Iraq in particular worked to create a genealogical system encompassing the entire Arabian Peninsula. As late as the early 800s, Maʿadd was often listed as the ultimate Arab ancestor, but at the same time, many started giving that honour to Ismaʿil (Ishmael), the son of Ibrahim who was driven into the wilderness. This made it easier to incorporate groups from the southern Arabian Peninsula who did not identify with Maʿadd, but were coming to be considered Arabs. These southerners claimed an ancestor named Qahtan, and together he and Maʿadd's father ʿAdnan came to be seen as the ancestors of two branches of the Arab people (Webb, 209–24).

According to another view, anyone who spoke Arabic was an Arab. Arabic originated perhaps three thousand years ago in the deserts of Jordan and northwestern Saudi Arabia, and subsequently spread elsewhere in the Arabian Peninsula, though large parts of the south still spoke other languages at the dawn of Islam. Classical Arabic as a literary language was developed through the work of grammarians in Basra and Kufa during the eighth and ninth centuries. These philologists developed the idea that the purest speech was that of the Bedouin, and so frequently consulted Bedouin or their immediate descendants in developing grammars and dictionaries. This led to a largely artificial construction which began the difference between a carefully learned elite language and various spoken dialects which persists in Arabic today. The elite language was originally constructed from a mishmash of various dialects.

Unfortunately, we have no inscriptions or other Arabic texts for eastern Arabia in the centuries immediately preceding the rise of Islam. What we do have, however, are Syriac Biblical commentaries of the seventh through tenth centuries containing glosses of certain difficult terms in the language of Beth Qatraye, which their authors recognized as distinct. The bulk of the vocabulary thus revealed is derived from Arabic, though Pahlavi (Middle Persian) and Syriac itself are also influences. An example is the use of "gmal ablaq" for a wingless locust, which seems related to the Arabic "jamal ablaq," or "piebald camel."[3] There is, however, nothing similar for other areas around the Gulf.

Conquered peoples began adopting Arabic as they were integrated into the society of the conquerors. For example, a Basran physician who lived in the early 700s was said to be the first Jew to write in Arabic, translating works from Syriac to Arabic on behalf of the Umayyad rulers in whose circles he circulated. In the early 800s, we see another stage of the language's penetration as part of a broader cultural mingling. At that time, one ʿAmmar of Basra wrote in Arabic, not as a translator or administrator, but as a Christian writing to other

---

3 Mario Kozah, "New Evidence for an Early Islamic Arabic Dialect in Eastern Arabia: The Qaṭrāyīth ("in Qatari") Spoken in Beth Qaṭraye," *Journal of Near Eastern Studies* 81 (2022): 71–83.

Christians, in this case objecting to the religious claims of Muslims. By the 900s, Arabic was becoming the main Christian language in the major cities of lower Iraq.[4]

Unfortunately, we have much less information on how Persians conceived of themselves during this period. Language, however, was probably an important factor, especially for those in contact with speakers of other languages. Several languages related to modern Persian were used in the early Islamic period. One, today called Pahlavi, was the elite literary language of the Sasanian Empire and the language of Zoroastrian texts and rituals. The language's script was also used for some of the writing on Azraqite coins. Southern Iran had its own spoken vernacular closely related to that literary language, and this was most likely the one used along the shores of the Persian Gulf. Modern Persian would evolve out of a version called Dari, which was originally the vernacular of regions further north and parts of what is now Iraq. This Dari, eventually written in modified Arabic script and with Arabic loanwords, would become modern Persian. Pahlavi continued in use for several centuries, however, turning up on some merchandise from an eighth-century shipwreck off Thailand and in inscriptions related to Persian merchants on India's Malabar coast in the late 800s.[5]

---

4 Gil, *Jews*, 297–98; Kevin van Bladel, "Arabicization, Islamization, and the Colonies of the Conquerors," in *Late Antique Responses to the Arab Conquests*, ed. Josephine van den Bent, Floris van den Eijnde, and Johan Weststeijn (Leiden: Brill, 2022), 89–119 at 101–2.

5 There is less work on the history of Persian than for Arabic, but elements of this paragraph come from Adam Gaiser, "What Do We Learn About the Early Khārijites and Ibāḍiyya from Their Coins?," *Journal of the American Oriental Society* 130 (2010): 167–87 at 175–76; John R. Perry, "New Persian: Expansion, Standardization, and Inclusivity," in *Literacy in the Persian World: Writing and the Social Order*, ed. Brian Spooner and William L. Hanaway (Philadelphia: University of Pennsylvania Museum of Archaeology and Anthropology, 2012), 70–94 at 72, 77; Gilbert Lazard, *The Origins of Literary Persian* (Bethesda: Foundation for Iranian

Even insofar as language can be a guide to identity, however, the picture in the early Islamic Gulf was much more complex than a simple focus on Arabic and Persian might indicate. Kumzari is a living language that reminds us of the complex linguistic picture once found around the Gulf. Today, it is spoken by a little over four thousand people in villages on the Musandam Peninsula and the nearby Iranian island of Larak. The language has Arabian roots, but a significant vocabulary traceable back to the Persian dialects of the Sasanian and early Islamic period, and from a separate stream to that which led to modern Persian. This makes the language very old, while also continually seasoned by new elements from populations which entered the Gulf over the centuries, such as the Portuguese.[6] As one might expect, it is critically endangered, with young people drifting heavily toward the more socially and economically useful Arabic and Persian.

Individuals could also shift in identity, as we see through the life of al-Muhallab b. Abi Sufra, the general who defeated the Azraqites and who was closely tied to the tribe of al-Azd. Al-Muhallab's father, a contemporary of Muhammad, was a Zoroastrian Persian from Kharg, perhaps a sailor, who moved to Oman and became a client of al-Azd and eventually a Muslim. Later, he became a horse

---

Studies, 1993), 35–37; John Guy, "The Phanom Surin Shipwreck, a Pahlavi Inscription, and Their Significance for the Early History of Lower Central Thailand," *The Journal of the Siam Society* 105 (2017): 179–96 at 188–91.

6 This paragraph synthesizes information from Christina van der Waal Anonby, "Traces of Arabian in Kumzari," *Supplement to the Proceedings of the Seminar for Arabian Studies* 44 (2014): 137–46; Erik John Anonby, "Kumzari," *Journal of the International Phonetic Association* 41 (2011): 375–80 at 375; Quentin Muller and Sebastian Castelier, "Last Stand of a Hybrid Language from Oman's Seafaring Past," *Middle East Eye*, October 4, 2016, https://www.middleeasteye.net/features/last-stand-hybrid-language-omans-seafaring-past.

groom for ʿUthman b. Abi al-ʿAs, a governor of Oman under one of the "rightly guided" caliphs who led the conquest of Fars and then settled in Basra. After al-Muhallab's victory against the Azraqites, he and his family became governors and military leaders along the eastern frontier in Central Asia. Their power base, however, remained the population of Oman, and the family was eventually equipped with a proper al-Azd genealogy tying them to Arabness. Of course, as noted above, al-Azd itself was not always accepted as an Arab grouping.

There were also languages and ethnicities once rooted in the Gulf, but long since absorbed into broader groupings. The inhabitants of Khuzistan were culturally distinct in the early Islamic period. As late as the end of the tenth century, they were conversant in both Arabic and Persian, but many also spoke another language descended from Elamite. According to a Basran writer named al-Jahiz, whom we will say more about below, it had a great variety of sounds and was difficult to learn. Muhammad was alleged to have said that it was the language of devils; although this tradition is certainly inauthentic, it does highlight the low status the Khuz had in the eyes of many litterateurs, who saw them as lowly and often treacherous. Due to immigration into Khuzistan from other areas, the Khuz proper gradually became most associated with the foothills of the mountains away from the Gulf shores.[7]

Africans and South Asians

Many today assume that South Asians and Africans came to the Persian Gulf only as guest workers in the days of oil, yet they have been present for centuries. Unlike the Arabs and Persians, their communities existed at the margins of mainstream culture, though individuals could become integrated,

---

7 Kevin van Bladel, "The Language of the Xūz and the Fate of Elamite," *Journal of the Royal Asiatic Society* 31 (2021): 447–62 at 449–53.

and women certainly became concubines. The emphasis on patrilineal genealogy in Arab society hides the fact, revealed by the modern study of genetics, that much of the population around the Gulf today has some ancestry from eastern Africa or India. A window into these populations' social position comes from the Basran writer al-Jahiz, whose grandfather was from sub-Saharan Africa.

In Late Antiquity, Syriac sources called part of lower Iraq Beth Hendwaye, with the second part of that term a cognate of the Arabic "al-Hind" for India. This may be connected with the group known as the Zutt, who were descendants of people from Sind, the region where the Indus River flows into the Arabian Sea, and relatives of the Jats who live today in Pakistan and northwestern India. During the early 400s, the Sasanians moved thousands of them from the southern Pakistani region of Sind to Khuzistan, where they settled along the Persian Gulf, ultimately expanding further along its shores and into Mesopotamia. In early Islamic times, they had their own quarter in Basra. At the same time, many used the marshes of lower Iraq and Khuzistan to maintain a buffalo herding lifestyle which they had brought from Sind. Under the Umayyads, many were also transferred to other regions of the Islamic Empire.[8]

The Zutt were not the only people the Sasanians brought from Sind. Another such group was the Sayabija, though their deeper origins probably lie in Southeast Asia, as their name is derived from that of an Indonesian island. Like the Zutt, they were part of Sasanian military garrisons around the Gulf. They also became clients of the Arab tribe of Tamim and wound up settled in Basra. Both Zutt and Sayabija were recruited by Basra's governors into security forces and as guards for key buildings such as the treasury, perhaps because they did

---

8 Patricia Crone, *Meccan Trade and the Rise of Islam* (Princeton: Princeton University Press, 1987), 47; Kristina Richardson, *Roma in the Medieval Islamic World: Literacy, Culture, and Migration* (London: I. B. Tauris, 2022), 22–24.

not have the tribal loyalties of the Arab inhabitants. In rural areas, the Sayabija also herded buffalo.[9]

These Sasanian deportees and their descendants were not the only inhabitants of the Gulf region of South Asian origin. Ships from South Asia definitely sailed the waters in or near the Persian Gulf, and at some point al-Ubulla had a temple for Indian gods. Pirates who were called *bawarij* after their ships are referenced in both poetry from the sixth century and historical accounts pertaining to the seventh and eighth; scholars believe they came from the coast of Pakistan. In the early 800s, *bawarij* activities led the Ibadi imamate in Oman to establish a navy which grew to several hundred ships. By the 700s, slaves from Sind were also frequently traded into the Islamic heartlands. During the 800s, Oman's Ibadi imam asked the governor of the port of Sohar to suppress a rebellion, which he did with the aid of a group of Indian mercenaries. According to one account, one mercenary risked his life to free some cattle from a burning enclosure.[10]

Those of sub-Saharan ancestry in the Gulf region were generally called the Zanj, and are best known today for a major revolt from 869 to 883. Although Muslim writers from the tenth century and later used the term "Bilad al-Zanj," or "Lands of the Zanj" to refer to Africa's Indian Ocean coast, ethnic and geographic terminology for that region was imprecise. Modern genetic studies and the names from our main account of the Zanj revolt indicate that most of the Zanj of the early Islamic Gulf were from either the upper Nile valley (Nubia and Ethiopia) or further west, in the lands bordering the Sahara. The Basran writer al-Jahiz, however, says there were also enslaved Zanj from an island called Qanbala, prob-

---

9 C. Edmund Bosworth, "Sayābidja," in *Encyclopaedia of Islam*, 2nd ed., 11 vols. (Leiden: Brill, 1954–2005), 9:97–98 is the standard description of this group.

10 For solid discussion of the *bawārij*, see Crone, *Meccan Trade*, 47; Eric Staples, "Oman and Islamic Maritime Networks, 630–1507 CE," in *Oman: A Maritime History*, ed. Abdulrahman Al Salimi and Eric Staples (Hildesheim: Olm, 2017), 81–115 at 88.

ably modern Pemba in Tanzania. The Zanj revolt accounts also reveal a complex linguistic situation in which many of the Zanj understood Arabic, but many did not, and required translators for the leader's speeches.

Both the Zutt and Zanj laboured in the marshes of southern Iraq where the Tigris and Euphrates emptied into the Persian Gulf. This region had fertile soil, but also a salty nitrous covering due to the high rate of evaporation. From at least the seventh century, labourers who were usually legally classified as slaves used to clear that topsoil and allow for cultivation. The results of this labour could still be seen in lower Iraq in the twentieth century, where saline ridges several metres high, formed of material long ago scraped off the surrounding agricultural land, extended over hundreds of square miles south of Basra west of the Shatt al-ʿArab, as well as along the east bank of the Tigris.[11]

The Zanj revolt of the late 800s was not the first uprising of the labourers around Basra. At the time of the Second Civil War, the Zanj, Zutt, and others in that area began plundering crops, and were suppressed as the war ended. Shortly after that end, however, they rose in a more organized revolt under the leadership of a man known by the moniker "Lion of the Zanj" in Persian who called himself "Commander of the Believers." They took control of some territory around al-Ubulla and defeated the first Umayyad army sent against them, but were themselves defeated shortly thereafter. Just a few decades before the largest Zanj revolt, the Zutt rose up and disrupted trade between Baghdad and Basra in a revolt lasting from 820 until 834.[12]

---

11 For the saline ridges, see Peter Verkinderen, *Waterways of Iraq and Iran in the Early Islamic Period: Changing Rivers and Landscapes of the Mesopotamian Plain* (London: I. B. Tauris, 2015), 73–75, 200; Richardson, *Roma*, 24, describes the legal status.

12 On these revolts, see ʿAbd al-Ameer ʿAbd Dixon, *The Umayyad Caliphate 65–86/684–704: A Political Study* (London: Luzac, 1971), 147–49.

The Zanj revolt which began in 869 was led by ʿAli b. Muhammad. He claimed to be a descendant of ʿAli, but the genealogy varied even as far as which son of ʿAli was involved. He was a panegyric poet in court circles in Samarra before leaving for al-Hasa in the early 860s. Many there came to believe he was a new prophet, and he appears to have set up a quasi-state in opposition to the Abbasid authorities. ʿAli gained a following in the city of Hajar before violence between his followers and opponents drove him to nearby al-Ahsa in the Hofuf Oasis, where further opposition caused him to withdraw into the desert. His Bedouin followers finally abandoned him after a military defeat. It was at this time that he later claimed to have had a vision urging him to go to Basra.

In Basra with a handful of followers from eastern Arabia, he proclaimed a revolt, but no one from the city joined them, and most of his followers and family were arrested. He fled to Baghdad, but returned to Basra a year later after his family was freed in a civil disturbance. After that, he took up residence in a small fortress on one of the canals near Basra. There, he encountered a Zanj slave named Rayhan b. Salih and learned of the harsh conditions in which they worked. ʿAli asked Rayhan for his loyalty and to recruit other Zanj, and when some had been recruited, ʿAli led the band to free groups of other Zanj slaves.

In addressing the freed Zanj, ʿAli recalled the poor conditions of their servitude and, casting himself as God's means of their deliverance, pledged to lead them to a prosperous future of owning their own slaves and homes (al-Tabari, 36–38). As his power grew, some villagers of the region, probably burdened by taxation, also supported his cause. Other villages, however, were plundered. Armed with rudimentary weapons, the Zanj army grew, including by recruiting Zanj from the Abbasid forces sent against them, and they began taking and burning cities, including the port of al-Ubulla. In 871, after recruiting a significant number of Bedouin from al-Hasa, they took Basra. In addition to the burning and pillaging of the city by Zanj-affiliated forces, one commander of a Bedouin contingent lured many inhabitants to a certain place under a promise of security, only to massacre them (al-Tabari, 126–28).[13]

In the wake of the fall of Basra, ʿAli b. Muhammad began sending commanders further afield, into Khuzistan and up to the northern edges of lower Iraq's marshes. Within the marshes, the rebels built settlements, collected taxes, and even minted their own coins. The largest settlement was their capital city of al-Mukhtara, which had a mosque, markets, judges and scribes, and mansions. However, the fall of Basra also led to the Abbasid prince al-Muwaffaq being given command of the war against the Zanj. Over the course of the 870s, he gradually eroded their power. In early 881 he laid siege to al-Mukhtara, eroding the defenders' morale by encouraging defectors, who were then incorporated into the Abbasid forces and honoured publicly in sight of the city. Finally, in summer 883, the city fell, and the rebellion was defeated.

ʿAli b. Muhammad's religious orientation cannot be neatly categorized. In addition to claiming descent from ʿAli b. Abi Talib, he called himself the Mahdi, and as we will see in chapter five this likely draws on Shiʿite eschatology. We also have coins, however, which feature slogans associated with the Shurat, as well as claiming that he was the grandson of an unnamed "Commander of the Believers."[14] The same slogans and claims were on his banner (al-Tabari, 38). He also claimed to have visions and miraculous knowledge guiding him, such as in his first move to Basra, and these included revelations of parts of the Qur'an which he said he did not previously know (al-Tabari, 36). In these ways, beyond his core Zanj following, he appealed to many who sought a religio-political alternative to the ruling Abbasids.

---

13 Parenthetical page numbers in this section are from Abū Jaʿfar Muḥammad b. Jarīr al-Ṭabarī, *The Revolt of the Zanj*, vol. 36 of *The History of al-Ṭabarī*, ed. and trans. David Waines, 40 vols. (Albany: State University of New York Press, 1992).

14 J. Walker, "A Rare Coin of the Zanj," *The Journal of the Royal Asiatic Society of Great Britain and Ireland* 3 (1933): 651–55 at 651–52.

ʿAli b. Muhammad's political goal was clearly the creation of an alternative society for his followers, justified by the abuse and corruption of the established order. Concerning the violence during Basra's fall, ʿAli b. Muhammad reported having a vision of an angel in the shape of a particular government official famous for torturing corrupt Abbasid officials to recover their ill-gotten gains. He also showed a keen interest in collecting the maximum amount of loot from the sack of the city, pushing aside commanders who were insufficiently zealous (al-Tabari, 133). It was this loot and other plunder gained from various raids that supported the Zanj settlements, effectively fulfilling the promise he made to his first followers.

In the racial constructions of the period, Zanj and Zutt were both often considered dark-skinned and faced prejudice at the hands of Arabs, Persians, and others. As noted, however, the ninth-century writer al-Jahiz, who spent much of his life in Baghdad but was born in Basra and died there just before the outbreak of the Zanj revolt, had Black ancestry, and among his writings is an epistle called *The Glory of the Blacks over the Whites* defending the honour of Blackness. In it, he recounts many famous Black figures of Arabian history and asserts that his readers are judging all Blackness from the menial labourers with which they are familiar. He was not a friend to the enslaved by any means, as he essentially grants the inferiority of Blacks from Qanbala, which he derides as a rural land of the uneducated, but says if they had met Blacks from Lanjawiyya, the African coast and interior, they would have a different impression.[15]

Al-Jahiz notes that before the early Islamic period, Arabs acknowledged intermarriage with Blacks in their ancestry. He also calls attention to the honour they afford to Black kings such as the Negus of Ethiopia, who in legend converted to Islam. Along with his contemporaries al-Jahiz believed in

---

15 Abu Uthman Amr b. Bahr al-Jahiz, *The Book of the Glory of the Black Race: Kitab Fakhr as-Sudan ʿala al-Bidan*, trans. Vincent Cornell (Los Angeles: Preston, 1981).

racial traits, and credited Blacks with generosity, natural dance rhythm, eloquence, and general niceness, as well as physical toughness and effort at manual labour. Of the colour black itself, he relates it to phrases in which it symbolized quality, as well as the fact that ebony was a highly prized wood. Black was often linked with beauty, such as in hair colour during one's youth, the pupils of the eye, and the use of kohl as a cosmetic.

Al-Jahiz's focus is mainly on African descent, but he does mention those of Indian ancestry, as well. He mentions cultural achievements of the Indian sub-continent, such as in mathematics, medicine, and the invention of chess. He also notes the singing ability of slave girls from Sind, as well as that people from there are best trusted to keep accounts and skilled in finance. Finally, he mentions that Sindi slaves were widely considered the best cooks. This is intriguing because South Asian cookware has been widely found around the Gulf shores and elsewhere in the region, believed to be for everyday use rather than a luxury item. The presence of this cookware and al-Jahiz's highlighting Sindi cooks could show South Asian influence on Gulf cuisine centuries ago.[16]

* * *

For the most part, scholars cannot be sure how much the ideas about ethnic characteristics articulated by literate elites in Baghdad and elsewhere were current in the Gulf in early Islamic times. However, linguistically, both Arabic and Persian were found mingled all along its shores, and ethnic identity could clearly be malleable. At the same time, the region was home to populations whose origins lay elsewhere in the Indian Ocean basin, populations which influenced the Gulf's history and culture. This calls to mind the region's economic links with a wider world, to which we will now turn.

---

16 Priestman, *Ceramic Exchange*, 1:192, 1:218.

Chapter 3

The Society of Trade in the Early Islamic Period

Sinbad the Sailor is often presented as a ship captain, and in the 2003 Dreamworks film was even a pirate. However, in classical Arabic the term *bahri* was used of anyone who travelled by sea, and The Arabian Nights character was actually a merchant who booked passage for himself and his goods for trading voyages. The framing of the tales is that a poor porter, also named Sinbad, discovers his namesake's luxurious home and muses that some continually struggle to get by when others live lives of such ease. Sinbad the Sailor hears the porter and summons him in to talk, and the tales are thus framed as a story of how the seafaring merchant earned his wealth through entrepreneurship and ingenuity amidst challenges earlier in life.[1]

Even though their present didactic form took shape later, the Sinbad stories come from a tradition of Indian Ocean tales that goes all the way back to ancient Egypt and Mesopotamia. We have a collection of such tales in the *Book of the Wonders of India*, attributed in later medieval times to an otherwise unknown Buzurg b. Shahriyar al-Ramhurmuzi, but compiled from Gulf informants by a Basran religious scholar named Abu ʿImran al-Sirafi and presented in 968 to a vizier

---

1 The interpretation of the Sinbad stories used in this book is that from *The Annotated Arabian Nights: Tales from 1001 Nights*, ed. and with an introduction by Paulo Lemos Horta, trans. Yasmine Seale (New York: Liveright, 2021), 201–62.

for the ruling dynasty of Egypt.[2] A similar book, though written more as an organized guide, is the *Accounts of China and India* which consists of updates and supplements made by one Abu Zayd al-Sirafi to an incorporated earlier text.

These stories focus on the dangers of the sea and distant lands, but also the wonders to be seen, and were a common folklore among the maritime classes. Their spread to other areas burnished the reputation of the great trading cities, much as did the wonders sometimes sent from them. In the early 900s, when the Abbasids ruled Sohar for a time, their governor there sent gifts of black gazelles, a golden statue of an Indian deity, and birds which spoke Sanskrit and Persian. To these were added more exotic legends such as an embalmed cat-sized ant from eastern Africa. Enabling the stories of such wonders, however, were everyday lives of labourers on ships and docks, in the making or collection of products, and producing the everyday essentials necessary for life.

Cities of Trade

In decades immediately before Islam, several annual market fairs were found along the Gulf coast. One of these was at al-Mushaqqar by a mountain in the Hofuf oasis.[3] This market was frequented by both Persians from Iran and caravans from Yemen and was supervised by Sasanian appointees from the Arabian tribe of Tamim. Shortly thereafter, a market took place at Dibba, a city which today is split between Oman and the United Arab Emirates. The Dibba fair was frequented by

---

2 Jean-Charles Ducène, "Une nouvelle source arabe sur l'Océan Indien au Xᵉ siècle: Le *Ṣaḥīḥ min aḫbār al-biḥār wa-ʿaǧāʾibihā* d'Abū ʿImrān Mūsā ibn Rabāḥ al-Awsī al-Sīrāfī," *Afriques* 6 (2015): unpag., https://doi.org/10.4000/afriques.1746.

3 The identification of al-Mushaqqar with the northwest of Jabal al-Qārah was made by ʿAbd al-Khāliq al-Janbī, *Hajar wa qaṣabātuhā al-thalāth: al-Mushaqqar – al-Ṣafā – al-Shabʿān, wa nahruhā Muḥallam* (Beirut: Dār al-Maḥajja al-Bayḍāʾ, 2004), 115–49.

merchants from India and Sind, as well as from further east. It was followed by a smaller, local fair at Sohar. The fairs at Dibba and Sohar were also under an Arabian appointee of the Sasanians, and those in charge at all three could collect taxes and sell their own merchandise first.

The early Islamic period, however, saw a new economic dynamism in the region linked to an increasing mobility of both people and wealth. As described in the first chapter, Arab garrison cities such as Basra were regional administrative centres into which poured revenue from the conquered territories. Arabs settled in these cities received cash stipends from the state, liquid wealth which could be used in commercial ventures involving one's tribal ties remaining in the Arabian Peninsula and along the Iranian coasts. By the eighth century, we have a burst of settlement along Kuwait Bay and the west coast of Qatar, to note just two regions which have been archaeologically surveyed.

In addition, the Umayyads and early Abbasids gradually reduced the degree to which the government set market prices, which had been routine under the Byzantines and Sasanians. Among the results of this was the creation of more extensive mercantile networks to find goods cheaply and transport them to places there they would command higher prices. One such network of Jewish merchants, the Radhaniyya, were named for "Radhan," which especially in Late Antiquity was the term applied to a large region of east central Iraq. As described by a writer from the mid-800s, their commercial networks extended from Spain to China based on land and sea routes, and trade in the goods from all these regions. In the Gulf, they traded particularly out of al-Ubulla towards Oman and on into the Indian Ocean.[4]

---

4 The link between government policy and merchant networks is argued by Fanny Bessard, *Caliphs and Merchants: Cities and Economies of Power in the Near East (700–950)* (Oxford: Oxford University Press, 2020), 212–13; Gil, *Jews*, 615–37 is the best study of the Radhaniyya.

As a maritime world, the Gulf's major hubs were port cities, but which port cities were most important has fluctuated over the centuries. The dominant Sasanian port in the Persian Gulf had been Rev Ardashir on the Bushehr Peninsula. Archaeological investigation has revealed the remains of a late Sasanian and early Islamic pier five metres wide and extending one hundred metres into the Gulf, part of an archaeological site of around 375 hectares (nearly 950 acres), with another 160 hectares nearby on the peninsula and another substantial settlement just across the bay. It is difficult to say when this settlement area developed, but it declined rapidly during the seventh and eighth centuries.

On the other hand, al-Ubulla, at the head of the Gulf, was the main port of Mesopotamia, not only under the Sasanians, but into the Islamic era, when it was called the "opening of India." It was also the site of one of the Middle East's two Indian Ocean-connected dockyards. Although Indian Ocean vessels could apparently reach it, the shallow water and uncertain channels of the Shatt al-Arab made navigation treacherous. During the tenth century, its approaches had small huts on palm tree trunks which had been stuck into the seabed, with men stationed at the huts to light signal fires to help ships find the channel and avoid whirlpools at night. Because of the navigational difficulties, small regional craft were used to ship goods to the major emporia of Siraf and Sohar, and may have been previously to Rev Ardashir.

The excavations at Siraf allow us an interesting look at a medieval Gulf port city. Located on a dry coastal plain only a single kilometre wide and four long, every scrap of available land was used by a population that may have reached 28,000. Because of its heat and aridity, water was brought from nearby mountain valleys to the city by conduits, open except where they passed through rock. These conduits were supplemented within the city by wells and rainwater cisterns. Siraf rose to prominence during the eighth century because the deep water of its harbour was suitable for ocean-going vessels, and soon became known for the wealth of its inhabitants and its general commercial prosperity. In the early

900s, customs dues at Siraf accounted for around fifteen per-cent of the total revenue of Fars.

Around 800, a large congregational mosque was built along its seafront, and the grand bazaar was on at least two and possibly all three of its remaining sides. The mosque may have held the city's official weights and measures and been otherwise associated with market regulation. The bazaar fea-tured many shops, a public bath, and one of the ten smaller mosques scattered around the city. The shops mainly had a single room, albeit with stands and cupboards, and at least one was a bakery. There was also a complex that may have been a caravanserai where visitors both stayed while in the city and displayed their own wares.

Siraf's excavations also highlight the existence of a class of large-scale traders and investors called by the Arabic word *tujjar*, which distinguished them from street vendors, shop-keepers, and travelling peddlers. This class arose during the eighth and ninth centuries as economic conditions under the caliphate favoured the rise of large merchant houses. By the time of the height of Siraf, they lived in neighbourhoods seg-regated from the general public, here along the slopes of the Zagros foothills forty-five metres (150 feet) above the level of the lower city with its much more modest dwellings. Travel accounts describe their mansions as having multiple storeys and built with teak and brick. One account from the mid-ninth century describes a particularly prominent Sirafi trader in Basra as having almost three million dinars' worth of assets.[5]

People of all the religions found in the Gulf were also found in Siraf, but the Zoroastrians have left the most evidence. A Zoroastrian high priest once travelled there to discuss a con-troversy with the community of his co-religionists in the city, and there are a number of large Zoroastrian ossuaries, as well as some references in the Arabic sources. Conversion to Islam was persistent, though, and even beyond the mosques we see signs of Islamic moral culture reflected archaeologi-

---

5 *Tujjār* as a class are discussed in Bessard, *Caliphs*, 247–53.

cally. The houses of the great merchants were designed for family privacy, such as with ground floor windows looking upon a central courtyard. Their stucco decorations featured geometric and vegetal patterns, as well as Qur'anic verses. In addition, small finds suggest that in contrast to much of Iran and Iraq, women wore their hair down and perhaps covered, a type of modesty that wasn't just associated with Islam.[6]

In contrast to Siraf, Sohar had abundant water resources, and served as a key provisioning station for ships leaving the Gulf. The ninth and tenth centuries saw a dramatic expansion of both the irrigation works in the countryside surrounding the city, as well as new conduits, both on the surface and underground, bringing water into it. Unlike in dry Siraf, these sometimes overflowed, causing flash flooding, and a particularly bad flood in 865 destroyed much of the city. The irrigation, however, provided food close to the city and even a surplus in dates which was exported as far as China. Through trade connections Soharis were also introduced to tropical fruits such as bananas and pomegranates which they also started to grow.[7]

Like Siraf, Sohar had both wealthy merchants, as well as a middle class and poorer residents. The merchants of Sohar built seaside mansions of gypsum, brick, and teak, with the wealthiest having rooves of ebony and aloe wood from Southeast Asia. It was also they who helped fund the city's public works. Most people, however, had smaller houses of palm fronds and branches. These were not a sign of destitution, as they were easily adapted to local conditions and a good use of natural resources. Fire was a danger, however, and on two

---

6 The Zoroastrian high priest's mission is from Averbuch, "From Siraf to Sumatra," 106–8; the observations on houses and islamization is from Bessard, *Caliphs*, 79, 249; and the connection to small finds and hair is from Simpson, "Nomads," 305.

7 In addition to Bryan Averbuch's dissertation, information on Sohar for this discussion comes from his chapter "Sohar: Forelands, Umland, and Hinterland in the History of an Omani Entrepot," in *The Ports of Oman*, ed. Al Salimi and Staples, 179–211.

Figure 1. Barasti houses made of woven date-palm
fronds in Fujairah, 1970s. Christine Osborne Pictures /
Alamy Stock Photo. Used with permission.

occasions in the 800s substantial portions of the city were
burned. Many jobs in Sohar were performed by enslaved
people, especially in agriculture, where their treatment was
bemoaned even by the ruling Ibadi imams.

Sohar also displayed religious and ethnic diversity. In
the tenth century, the traveller and geographer al-Muqaddasi reported that although Arabic was spoken in the lands
around it, Sohar's own lingua franca was Persian, and many
people from Siraf had moved there when both cities were
ruled by the Buyids. The enslaved population came mostly
from Africa and South Asia, and there were merchants and
seafarers from around the Indian Ocean. Among the merchants there were also Jews and Zoroastrians, and it was
actually a Zoroastrian who built one of the city's most famous
water channels. Like Siraf, Sohar had a seaside mosque next
to its bazaar.

During the ninth century, the Ibadi imams who ruled
Oman developed an Islamic jurisprudence to match Sohar's
maritime economy. Although religious leaders from Oman's

interior disapproved of earning a living at sea, their works are nonetheless filled with discussions of shipwreck and salvage rights, how one performed the required daily prayers with their ritualized prostrations on ships that might be in rough waters, how conflicts with pirate ships fit into the Islamic law of war, and rights to goods which washed up on shore. One ruling discusses what to do if a merchant has reserved cargo space on another's ship, but then changes his mind at an early port of call. If unloading the goods would involve too much delay, someone aboard ship would be appointed as agent in charge of them and the captain would still be responsible for their safe transport.[8]

Oman had what were effectively trade agreements with realms in South Asia and East Africa, with each party granting security to the others' merchants and agreeing to tax them at the same rate. The religious authorities forbid Ibadis from permanently basing themselves in non-Muslim lands, but traders generally ignored this. Those who were not Muslims or People of the Book were confined to Sohar, which is also where trade goods were taxed. Muslims trading in Sohar paid only the very light zakat tax of 2.5 percent on cash and a set monetary value on livestock that was held for an entire taxation year. No taxes were levied on Muslim goods held in the country less than a year if they were in transit to another Muslim land, though goods in transit between non-Muslim lands were taxed. Many luxury products, such as pearls and frankincense, were not taxed at all until actually exchanged for something. These tax rates were doubled for Christians, who also paid the head tax, while the source mentions a different taxation regime for Jews without going into detail.

---

8 Some of this is mentioned in Wilkinson, *Ibâḍism*, 297–300, but the major discussion is J. C. Wilkinson, "Ṣuḥār (Sohar) in the Early Islamic Period: The Written Evidence," in *South Asian Archaeology, 1977: Papers from the Fourth International Conference of the Association of South Asian Archaeologists in Western Europe*, ed. M. Taddei, 2 vols. (Naples: Instituto Universitario Orientale, 1979), 888–907.

Ships and Journeys

The modern English word "dhow" refers to many different types of boats and ships in the western Indian Ocean, though such a collective term has not historically been used in the region itself. Instead, there have been a great variety of terms for different vessels based on size and function, and contrary to impressions, much innovation and change over time, even in the medieval period. The most distinctive characteristic of such ships is the fact that they were sewn together, often with fibre from coconut husk or date palm trees. Sewing provided the hull with greater resilience and allowed for easier repairs than would iron nails, though there are references to occasional use of wooden nails. Seams between the planks were caulked, often with rope mixed with fish or coconut oil.

Other characteristics simply highlight the differences among dhows and their variation over time. Most ships had only small fore and aft decks, but plenty did have full decks, and other small craft may have had none. Goods were stowed carefully and tightly and then covered with hide, matting, or perhaps palm fronds or simple planking on which the crew worked and lived. Ships had square-rigged sails on masts to provide stability and make full use of the following monsoon winds, though there is some evidence that lateen sails may have had some role. Ships could also have animal head stems, perhaps related to ancient ideas of guardian spirits or an evolution from animal sacrifices before a voyage.

In 1998, fishermen off the coast of an island called Belitung just east of Sumatra in Indonesia discovered a sunken ship probably originally from the Persian Gulf and bearing a cargo of mostly intact Chinese pottery. This discovery shows a fascinatingly integrated world of Indian Ocean commerce. Much of the wood for the ship's construction was from Africa: mahogany for the frame and hull planking and juniper for the cargo planks. The through-beams, however, were made of teak from India. The anchor, meanwhile, had a wooden shank with an iron grapnel, and assuming the iron was cast, would have been a product of China.[9]

The remnants of the twine used to sew the Belitung shipwreck have been difficult to study, but it may include a type of hibiscus found in China and Southeast Asia. The wadding has also been tentatively identified as paperbark from Southeast Asia's marshlands. If these identifications are correct, then they show that the ship underwent maintenance in Southeast Asia or perhaps southern China, and in fact such ships underwent continuous maintenance during voyages. Some of the artifacts from the ship were also from Southeast Asia, either acquired by the crew there, or perhaps brought aboard by new crew.

A designated cook among the crew baked unleavened bread, while fish predictably were another staple of the diet on board. A pestle and mortar, rolling pin, and fishing weights were all found in the Belitung wreckage. Passengers, however, could cook for themselves. According to a twelfth-century compendium of Ibadi law, water in a ship's main water tank belonged collectively to all on board, with a designated crew member managing its distribution to individuals who had their own smaller vessels. Wealthy passengers often brought their own water, as well. Seawater was sufficient for prayer ablutions. Water could also be drained from coconuts, which were imports in the Middle East, but plentiful in some of the regions sailors would visit.

Ships were crowded, and passengers had to remain seated so as not to get in the crew's way. Some did have compartments for passengers and slaves under a main deck and above the main cargo areas, though these had a reputation as unpleasant places to travel. More pleasant would be tents or pavilions constructed on the main deck, or even directly on stored cargo, allowing for privacy with fresh air. The earliest

---

9 This paragraph and the next are based on the analysis of Michael Flecker, "The Origin of the Tang Shipwreck: A Look at its Archaeology and History," in *The Tang Shipwreck*, ed. Chong and Murphy, 35–37.

references to such compartments were for women, and their appearance may have been part of the same Islamization of material culture seen in Siraf's houses.

Products

While the long-distance luxury trade was most famous, the bulk of goods shipped around the Persian Gulf were more mundane goods traded regionally. According to a recent analysis, depending on the time and place, between 25 percent and 50 percent of pottery found at Persian Gulf archaeological sites came from elsewhere in the Persian Gulf, rather than being either local to the site or from further afield. This is a clear testimony to the region's unity, a mobility of goods to go with the mobility of people, and an interdependence such that what happened in one area could have an impact on the daily life of others.[10]

Pottery, however, could also be shipped over long distances. Basra and its hinterland was also the source of kilns producing ceramics for long distance trade, and such wares have been found as far afield as Japan and included among the cargo, not only of the Belitung shipwreck, but another Middle Eastern ship off Thailand and a Southeast Asian one near Vietnam, both of which date from the late 700s. The Belitung shipwreck also contained several dishes made in China, but featuring motifs inspired by Iran and blue colouring from Iranian cobalt, thus showing the wide integration of the production and marketing of such items. To further tighten the web, cheaper versions of those Chinese wares were made around Basra, achieving the glistening white of the Chinese by using local yellow clay and adding a white glaze.[11]

---

10 The analysis was in Priestman, *Ceramic Exchange*, 1:218.

11 John Guy, "Hollow and Useless Luxuries: The Tang Shipwreck and the Emerging Role of Arab Traders in the Late First Millennium Indian Ocean," 167–68, 171, 175 and Stephen Murphy, "Asia in the Ninth Century: The Context of the Tang Shipwreck," 12–20 at 17–18, both in *The Tang Shipwreck*, ed. Chong and Murphy; Tim

Textiles were also widely traded, and several places around the Gulf were known for their cloth products. Basra was famous for its cotton and silk exports. Embroidered garments were among the most valuable, and one writer wrote of seeing in Basra cloaks with floral designs. Al-Ubulla, more a transit point than a manufacturing centre, still produced widely appreciated turbans. Khuzistan had many cloth centres, and the province's capital was a major exchange centre for the trade linked to Basra. In the late tenth century, several small ports of Fars had embroidered textile factories founded by the Buyids, who came to rule the region in the tenth century. One specific product mentioned from the region was napkins with a velvety surface which were exported all over the world.[12]

Tawwaj, located near the Bushehr Peninsula, became particularly famous, even though most garments named after it came to be made in Kazerun, on the caravan route connecting Siraf and Shiraz. In Tawwaj, the linen was made from flax fibres, which were tied into stalks and put in water tanks, which separated the fibre from the material used for threads. The threads were then washed in a water channel which turned them white; this water channel was owned by the Buyids themselves, who ran the cloth production industry. Government officials certified the amount and quality of bales of cloth, which were then sold directly to merchants.[13]

Pearls were the main commodity from the Gulf which was in demand across Eurasia, and today they are frequently highlighted as important to the region's heritage. They were used as jewelry, and their pure white colour led to their play-

---

Stanley, "Patterns of Exchange in the Decorative Arts between China and South-west Asia," in *Aspects of the Maritime Silk Road: From the Persian Gulf to the East China Sea*, ed. Ralph Kauz (Wiesbaden: Harrassowitz, 2010), 107–15.

12 R. B. Serjeant, *Islamic Textiles: Material for a History up to the Mongol Conquest* (Beirut: Librarie du Liban, 1972), 36–38, 40–47, 49–54.

13 Serjeant, *Islamic Textiles*, 52.

ing a role in Christian symbolism which in early Islamic times the Church of the East carried as far as China. While pearl fisheries were found elsewhere, connoisseurs considered those of the Gulf to have the best quality. Within the Gulf, the main pearl fisheries were found around Bahrain, Kharg, and Kish, and more generally in the southern Gulf from al-Hasa to the Musandam Peninsula near the Arabian coast, where the waters are shallower than on the Persian side.

A diver's perspective on pearling is found in poetry prob-ably written by the pre-Islamic poet al-Musayyib b. ʿAlas, though it is sometimes attributed to the nephew who trans-mitted his lines, Maymun b. Qays, known as al-ʿAsha, and who died during the 620s. It refers to a small crew of four from diverse backgrounds striving together against the elements, earning little reward. The successful dive is then described:

Then plunged he, long and lithe, his hair a shock /
his teeth clenched firm, determined to brave the worst
He then unclenched, spitting oil from his mouth, and groped, /
athirst, his heart ablaze with the fire of need;
This need had slain his father: he said, And I /
will follow his road, or win to the World's Desire.
Full half a day the waters covered him up /
his comrades knew not what he wrought in the deep;
Then won he his longed-for prize, and upward he bore /
the Pearl in its shell, that shone like a burning coal.[14]

Although divers could be in business for themselves, more common was working for someone else who financed the dive in exchange for the pearl catch. In Sasanian times this could

---

[14] The translation is mostly from Charles J. Lyall, "The Pictorial Aspects of Ancient Arabian Poetry," *Journal of the Royal Asiatic Society of Great Britain and Ireland* (January 1912), 133–52 at 146–47, though I have made some adjustments based on ʿAbd Allāh Yūsuf al-Ghunyam, *Kitāb al-Luʾluʾ*, 2nd ed. (Kuwait City: A.Y. al-Ghunaym, 1998), 15–16. The poem's authorship is discussed in Charles J. Lyall, "The Pearl-Diver of al-Aʾsha," *Journal of the Royal Asiatic Society of Great Britain and Ireland* (April 1912), 499–502.

be an agent for the imperial court, which might have claimed the choicest pearls for its own purposes. Others would then be traded through a pearl market at Rev Ardashir. Christians were definitely involved in this trade, and one pearling supervisor even became catholicos. In 585, Catholicos Ishoyahb I addressed the question of whether pearl divers could work or travel on a Sunday, saying that they could not do so voluntarily, but made allowance if they were under constraint. In Islamic times, funding pearling expeditions became the preserve of individual merchants.

Some pearls fetched outstanding prices and became exceptionally famous. It seems likely that several pearls were called Durr Yatimah, one of which was found near Kharg and owned by the Umayyad caliph Hisham in the early 700s. It was said to have perfect roundness and lustre and a mass of over 12 grams. When the Abbasids came to power, it was sent to Mecca. Its value of 120,000 dinars during the early 900s was, in a 2012 book, calculated at the equivalent to 15.5 million U.S. dollars. Around 800, a sponsor of pearling expeditions sold two pearls for a combined 100,000 dinars to the Abbasid caliph Harun al-Rashid and retired to Oman a wealthy man. More commonly, the smallest, weighing less than a gram, would sell for two to three dinars.[15]

The biggest long-distance imports to the Gulf were the spices and aromatics for which the Indian Ocean trade is most famous. Cloves, nutmeg, pepper, and mace added to the taste of food and served as expensive medications in the pharmacological theories of the time. Camphor and ambergris, too, were medicinal products and food additives. Camphor and aloe wood were also burned for pleasant smells, not unimportant in an age before deodorant. They were also used in soaps. Such luxuries became a key attribute of the lifestyle of both the rulers and the elite traders.

---

15 The price calculation and discussion is from Robert Carter, *Sea of Pearls*, 36–37, 44.

In addition to its luxury uses, camphor also became a crucial part of preparing corpses for burial in Islam, a development which shows that the Gulf was not incidental to the development of the broader religious tradition. Hadith originating in Basra describe how, when Muḥammad's daughter died, he instructed that she be washed with water and the ground leaves from the lote tree, after which she be treated with camphor to restore her complexion. Lote trees are found in the oases of eastern Arabia, and they are prominent in the Qur'an's depiction of paradise. This hadith found its way into influential collections, and so spread throughout the Islamic world.[16]

Mention must also be made of the slave trade. By the tenth century, Oman's traders were the most famous slave dealers. As noted previously, slaves were often put to agricultural labour, including in Oman itself. Women were also enslaved sexually and as entertainers; According to al-Jahiz, South Asian concubines were particularly sought after in Basra. Stories of the slave trade in the *Book of the Wonders of India* are surprisingly frank. In one, a sailor tells of how they were about to leave a Southeast Asian island with a cargo of slaves begging for mercy, with the crew uncaring. In that case, the slaves overpowered the few guards left on board, taking the ship and stranding the crew. Crews not caring about slaves' desire for freedom also comes up in other tales.

Traders in Religion and Politics

A history of the early Ibadis fancifully attributed to an early Ibadi leader in that city recounts how prominent Basran traders supported and played leadership roles in the movement. One of them from the mid-700s, Abu ʿUbayda ʿAbd Allah b. al-Qasim, initially came from a small market town in Oman before becoming rich in the trade with China. An ethical man

---

16 Leor Halevi, *Muhammad's Grave: Death Rites and the Making of Islamic Society* (New York: Columbia University Press, 2007), 53–54.

who ended partnerships with business partners whom he saw as unscrupulous, he studied Ibadi thought and traditions, and ultimately relocated to Mecca. Later, around 800, two Ibadi leaders were from the same family as another prominent trader, who seems to have been among the merchants who helped finance the early Ibadis' teaching and military movement.[17]

The commercial classes of the great cities also looked out for their economic interests when politics threatened to impinge on it. As described in the *Book of the Wonders of India*, in the days of Abbasid rule in Sohar, a Jewish merchant named Ishaq was based there, but after a dispute with one of his co-religionists, left for India. He came back with far more wealth than he had had previously, and bribed the governor to avoid the customs dues. Someone turned him in to the caliph, however, who sent men to seize Ishaq and take the taxes. The governor complied, but informed the other traders of the city. Fearing that all their fortunes could be at risk from future attention from Baghdad, they closed the markets and sent petitions to the governor protesting that his actions would result in ships avoiding Sohar in the future. The caliph's men extracted only a paltry sum from Ishaq, who then fled.

* * *

In an era when the bulk of all economic production was agricultural, the Gulf stood out for its emphasis on seaborne trade, most dramatically the long-distance trade around the Indian Ocean and as far as China. Pearls, textiles, and pottery were among the most significant items in this trade, which also included the misery and exploitation of the slave trade. This trade, however, was not constant and unchanging, as the next chapter will show.

---

17 Wilkinson, *Ibâḍism*, 163, 176, 180; Monik Kervran, "Famous Merchants of the Arabian Gulf in the Middle Ages," *Dilmun: Journal of the Bahrain Historical and Archaeological Society* 11 (1983): 21–24.

Chapter 4

New Trade Centres after 1000

Today the preeminent Gulf emporium is Dubai in the United Arab Emirates. A hub for air transit, corporate operations, and retail tourism, it has an impressive number of five-star hotels as well as the world's tallest building. Elsewhere in the region, Doha, Qatar's capital, hosted the 2022 FIFA World Cup as part of its bid for prominence, while Kuwait City, Abu Dhabi, and Manama are among the other cities with multicultural populations and a good deal of international commerce passing through. However, none of them existed before the 1700s, and even then most existed only as small fishing villages or centres of significance mainly for their own local areas.

Their rise fits a pattern of Gulf trade centres appearing and thriving, only to later be eclipsed by newcomers. Often, the fate of Gulf ports was determined by political fortunes and competition. Today's most important entrepots owe their significance mainly to the backing of an oil economy, but also to an independence enabled by their rulers' alliance with the British during a period in which neighbours sought to absorb them. The tenth century and later saw a fracturing of political authority which led to economic and even military competition over trade routes and revenues. This competition weighs against assertions that conflicts over trade in the Indian Ocean basin only became violent with the coming of the Portuguese and other Western Europeans. While it is true that, because of the scale of the Indian Ocean, no power sought to control its entire littoral, polities for whom trade was significant would fight for mercantile prominence in smaller areas.

Shifting Patterns of Trade

Scholars used to believe that disturbances in the Gulf region during the tenth century and the wealth and power of the Fatimid dynasty in Egypt led to a shift in Indian Ocean trade from the Persian Gulf to the Red Sea. However, although there is clear evidence of decline near the beginning of this period, and Siraf and al-Ubulla had passed their peak, new entrepots arose in the lower Gulf. Trade in the region was further enhanced by rulers of a Central Asian nomadic background who promoted long-distance trade and allied with the great trading families, the elite of which became even wealthier and held more power than those from previous centuries. It is probably during this period that the Sinbad stories began taking something like the form we have them in today.

The Zanj revolt described in chapter two was but one of a series of devastating wars fought around the head of the Gulf during the late ninth and into the tenth centuries. As the Abbasid government lost control of more of its territories, southern Iraq and Khuzistan became a battleground for rival claimants to influence and local powers seeking to maintain and expand their domains. In the second quarter of the 900s the Buyids, mentioned in the introduction and chapter three, united most of Iran and Iraq and restored a modicum of order, but with a diminished agricultural base. Princes of that dynasty, however, would also fight among themselves for prominence, so periods of stability in many areas were short.

The tenth century also saw the rise of the Qarmatians. Based in al-Hasa, they had their own unique religious doctrines, as will be described in chapter five which discusses Islamic sects. They also, however, caused major disruptions to trade in the region. They threatened Basra, resulting in merchants avoiding the head of the Gulf, and at one point even tried to claim both Basra and Khuzistan. They also raided Oman's ports and coastal towns in Fars. Their objective seems to have been tribute, as they don't seem to have had a clear sense of how to govern a commercial economy. They made attacks on pilgrim caravans to Mecca, probably to replace income the Bedouin lost when the Abbasids lost the ability to maintain and protect the pilgrimage routes using their labour. Finally, in 939, they reached an agreement with the Abbasids to protect pilgrimage caravans for an annual stipend.[1]

Such events contributed to a major decline in settlement and economic exchange in the Gulf during the tenth and eleventh centuries. Although Iraq was a significant source of ceramics for the Indian Ocean basin in earlier times, we find fewer of its wares from sites after 1000. In the mid-eleventh century, the traveller Nasir-i Khusraw wrote of it, "When I arrived, most of the city lay in ruins, the inhabited parts being greatly dispersed, with up to half a league from one quarter to another."[2] Of Tawwaj's cloth trade, we learn that the decline of Buyid authority in the early 1000s meant that fraud became rife and merchants avoided it. Several sites seem to have been abandoned, such as Bilad al-Qadim on Bahrain and Murwab along the coast of Qatar, and Sohar in Oman also declined. Much of southern Khuzistan, was also depopulated, and the cities further inland became its main centres.[3]

Although the Buyids began the process of trying to secure a new maritime prosperity based on the lower Gulf, the true

---

1 István Hajnal, "Some Aspects of the External Relations of the Qarāmiṭa in Baḥrayn," in *Fortresses of the Intellect: Ismaili and Other Studies in Honour of Farhad Daftary*, ed. Omar Ali-de-Unzaga (London: I. B. Tauris, 2011), 227–60 at 232–37. The possible motive for attacks on hajj caravans comes from Salīḥ b. Sulaymān al-Nāṣir al-Washmī, *al-Athār al-ijtimāʿiyya wa-al-iqtiṣādīyya li-ṭarīq al-ḥājj al-Irāqī ʿalā mintaqa al-Qaṣīm* (Beirut: Muʾassasa al-Risāla, 1994), 96–97.

2 Nasir-i Khusraw, *Nasir-i Khusraw's Book of Travels*, ed. and trans. Wheeler M. Thackston (Costa Mesa: Mazda, 2001), 116.

3 The site abandonments are described in Verkinderen, *Waterways*, 141; Tawwaj's cloth trade in Serjeant, *Islamic Textiles*, 52.

revival of commerce in the region would come with the Seljuqs. A family of Ghuzz Turks, they were part of a significant Turkish migration into Iraq and Iran during the eleventh century and became rulers from as far as Syria back into Central Asia. In 1055, they entered Baghdad and received legitimation from the Abbasid caliph. Following Central Asian political traditions, prominent members of the family each had their own territory, while recognizing one of their number as their common overlord. Most significantly for us, the dynasty promoted long-distance trade throughout their domains, probably a legacy of their roots among the trade routes of Central Asia.

The lower Gulf would be unified politically under a branch of the Seljuq family beginning with Qavurd Khan, son of one of the two brothers who led the family into the Middle East. ("Khan" here is a title following the name, as is "Shah" in "Malik Shah" below.) In the late 1040s Qavurd took Kirman, and after consolidating his power there, moved south to take the coasts along the Gulf of Oman and Strait of Hormuz, establishing order under his rule among feuding groups of nomads and the remnants of older dynasties. Finally, in the 1050s, he moved on to Oman, where he occupied the coast while occasional making forays inland to defend his possessions.

Within this domain, Qavurd Khan worked to build the infrastructure for long-distance trade. He developed the harbour at Makran's port of Tiz and built caravansarais and road bridges to facilitate the caravan routes through Makran's "Green Belt" of valleys, as well as watchtowers and other fortifications to defend their security. The same policy was followed in Oman. It was also in these coastal domains that Qavurd spent much of his time. In 1073, he was killed when he sought to become head of all Seljuq domains in place of his nephew Malik Shah; however, Malik Shah continued his policies, and even allowed Qavurd's descendants to continue as governors.

The blossoming of the lower Gulf during the Seljuq period is seen with new settlements appearing both archaeologically and in texts. There is an increase in known sites on the island of Qeshm, including small harbours and workshops. Settlements also appear on Oman's coastal plain. Qalhat appears as a new port in Oman, and we also have the first mention of Julfar near modern Ras al-Khaimah north of Dubai. Sites around the Indian Ocean basin also show that most pottery from the Gulf was now coming from southern Iran, where they obtained something like the whiteness of Chinese pottery by introducing quartz powder into the clay. Julfar, meanwhile, became a source for pottery traded within the Gulf region.[4]

The Rise of Kish

Kish, known in Arabic as Qays, would become the most important of these new ports and one famous for the use of violence in competition over trade. A coral island nineteen kilometres (twelve miles) south of the Iranian mainland, it is about fifteen kilometres long and eight wide. The origins of Kish's population and ruling family are obscure. Different accounts mention rulers migrating with their people from Syria and Yemen, the island was at one point known as a base for people of South Asian origin, and there is evidence the inhabitants may simply have been from the Persianized Arabs of that region. Geographers do report that the population was mainly Arab, which could be a result either of migration or of non-Arabs taking on Arab genealogies.

Kish used naval power to displace Siraf as the Gulf's most import port. Siraf had been struck in 977 by a destructive earthquake, which the late tenth-century geographer al-Muqaddasi attributed to the sins of fornication and usury.

---

4 Priestman, *Ceramic Exchange*, 1:195; Stanley, "Patterns," 111; Nasser Saʿid ʿAli al-Jahwari, *Settlement Patterns, Development, and Cultural Change in the Northern Oman Peninsula* (Oxford: BAR Publishing, 2013), 172–73; Alireza Khosrowzadeh, "The Second Season of the Archaeological Season of the Qeshm Island, Iran," *Iranian Journal of Archaeological Studies* 4 (2014), 21–39 at 34; Timothy Power, "Julfar and the Ports of Northern Oman," in *The Ports of Oman*, ed. Al Salimi and Staples, 219–44 at 223–24.

Several years later it was rebuilding, but the scale would not be the same. During the eleventh century, ships from Kish harassed ships en route to Siraf to force them to put in at Kish, instead. The city's Seljuq governor occasionally sent fleets to stop Kish, but accepted bribes to relent. Siraf declined into an entrepot of only local significance, and the city's last dated tombstones and monuments are from the 1100s. By the 1200s, it was mostly ruins with a silted up harbour, and a Sirafi diaspora had spread around the Western Indian Ocean.

Kish used its navy aggressively, diverting trade from Sohar the same way it had from Siraf. It also attacked ports of western India, whose people fought back using dugout canoes. One well-documented attack was a blockade of the Yemeni port of Aden 1135. With fifteen ships carrying about seven hundred men it prevented access to Aden and so controlled the entrance to the Red Sea for about two months. After that, two ships of a merchant named Ramisht arrived and successfully ran the blockade. The defenders then sent some of their troops on those ships to challenge the besiegers, who, having already run short of supplies, retreated. The motive of this blockade may have been to divert traffic to a nearby Yemeni port under Kish's control.[5]

In 1154, Kish turned its attention to Bahrain. For around a century at that point, the island and al-Hasa had been ruled by a family confederation of the ʿUyunids, named for the oasis where they were landlords before displacing the Qarmatians in alliance with the Seljuqs. Kish's first attempt at conquest resulted in defeat and the king's brother being taken captive, but control of Bahrain and its access to the pearl banks alternated frequently in the later 1100s before Kish was able to

---

5 The attack is analyzed in Roxani Eleni Margariti, "Mercantile Networks, Port Cities, and 'Pirate' States: Conflict and Cooperation in the Indian Ocean World of Trade before the Sixteenth Century," *Journal of the Economic and Social History of the Orient* 51 (2008): 543–77 at 559–61.

impose tribute amounting to as much of two-thirds of ʿUyunid revenue and direct control over some islands and villages.

Kish not only took Siraf's trade, but many of the traders themselves simply moved to the island as the new regional entrepot. It also had commercial links with Shiraz and other cities in Fars. The mostly stone ruins of Harireh, Kish's main medieval settlement, are found west of the modern port along a three-kilometre stretch of the island's north coast and extend about one kilometre inland. Next to a fortress there was a pier and anchorage with a structure featuring sea stairs and what may have been workshops. There was also a mosque and water cisterns, as well as the remains of several underground water channels, one of which is now a tourist attraction misleadingly billed as an "underground city."[6]

New Powers in the Thirteenth Century

Much as Kish had risen to prominence through military engagements aimed at controlling trade, so it would in the thirteenth century fall victim to the violence of others. At the same time, the overall volume of trade continued to increase, as the Seljuqs would ultimately give way to the Mongols. In the 1300s Kish would face its final defeat at the hands of Hormuz, which then occupied an island in the Strait of Hormuz controlling access to the Persian Gulf. At the beginning of the 1200s however, Hormuz was a port on the Iranian coast of mostly regional significance as the emporium of Kirman. What it did have was a fleet, and as early as 962 it leased it to support the Buyid invasion of Oman. In the 1200s, it would ally with the power which soon displaced Kish, a dynasty called the Salghurids.

A Turkish dynasty, the Salghurids came to power in 1148 during a power vacuum in Fars, but shortly thereafter paid allegiance to the Seljuqs, and later their successors in the

---

6 A detailed description is in Irāj Afshār (Sīstānī), *Jāzīreh Kīsh va Daryā-yi Pārs* (Tehran: Jahān-i Moʿāṣir, 1991), 78, 209–18.

region. Their move into becoming a true Gulf power came under Abu Bakr, whose reign began in 1226. He lacked a navy, but made an alliance with the ruler of Hormuz to support an invasion of Kish, for which the port power would receive a third of its revenue. As part of this support, he prevented inhabitants of the coastal regions from fighting on behalf of Kish. In 1229, Hormuz seized the island and massacred the royal family. Despite the agreement with Abu Bakr, however, the Hormuzi sovereign decided to keep the entrepot for himself.[7]

Because of this, Abu Bakr banned ports under his control from doing business with Hormuz and spent the next year developing a navy. In this he was aided by two of Kish's traders. He then conquered Kish for himself and killed the ruler of Hormuz. This marked the end of Kish's independence, as it would be under Salghurid rule until 1272. Many of the island's prominent residents had relocated to Shiraz in the aftermath of Hormuz's invasion and, given much of the capital supporting its trade was based in Fars as Siraf's had been, rule from that region was undoubtedly seen as reasonable, especially as the Salghurids made major investments on the island.

Over the next fifteen years, Abu Bakr would also conquer Bahrain and al-Hasa, including the offshore islands. In order to prevent raids the Salghurids wound up paying a tribute in dates to the ʿUqaylids, Bedouin rulers who were in the late stages of displacing the ʿUyunids. A sign of Salghurid investment on Bahrain is the redevelopment of an ancient fortress as a commercial emporium, and a village developed around it including its own market and public baths. Excavations at the fortress-turned-emporium show rooms repaired and renovated into warehouses for Chinese goods, as well as workshops for making date honey.[8]

---

7 This paragraph and the next are a combination of Ralph Kauz, "The Maritime Trade of Kish during the Mongol Period," in *Beyond the Legacy of Genghis Khan*, ed. Linda Komaroff (Leiden: Brill, 2006), 51–67, esp. 56–57 with Piacentini Fiorani, *Beyond Ibn Hawqal's Bahr al-Fārs*, 151.

8 For the fortress-turned-emporium, see Monik Kervran, Fredrik

Abu Bakr's influence was such that he had the nominal allegiance of rulers even as far as India, but the Salghurids would quickly be displaced by the new rising power in Asia, the Mongols. At the same time as he was expanding, Abu Bakr had identified the descendants of Chinggis Khan as the new power to whom he should pay allegiance, and thus sent his nephew to the Mongol court with tribute, receiving in return the Mongol title of Qutlugh Khan. Within a generation, however, the Mongols had set aside the Salghurid descendants and ruled Fars and its former dependencies directly. The last Salghurid was Abu Bakr's granddaughter, Abish Khatun, who died in confinement in 1284 but received a Mongol burial.[9]

The Mongols would bring the Persian Gulf trade to new heights. Especially after 1279, when Qubilai conquered southern China, the sea lanes became the main connecting routes between Mongol-ruled China and the Ilkhanate, as the Mongol rule of Iran is known. Like the Seljuqs, the Mongols were familiar with the caravan routes of Central Asia and the administration of commerce. In fact, Mongol elites even participated in trade themselves by funding the ventures of merchants via the *ortoq* system, in which they received a portion of the proceeds generated from their capital. The Mongols also developed a consumer culture and taste for the luxury goods which had long been traded across the Indian Ocean.

All these migrations and wars also impacted the ethnic diversity of the Gulf, adding new groups to the mix described in chapter two and further enriching the region's culture. Although the earliest rulers of Kish claimed Arab descent, by 1200 one account described the king as a Persian who dressed in Daylamite clothing, which had become prestigious under the Buyids. The Middle Eastern practice of militaries

Hiebert, and Axelle Rougeulle, *Qalʿat al-Bahrain: A Trading and Military Outpost, 3rd Millennium B.C.–17th Century A.D.* (Turnhout: Brepols, 2005), 283–89, 329–32.

9 Peter Jackson, *The Mongols and the Islamic World: From Conquest to Conversion* (New Haven: Yale University Press, 2017), 245–46, 266, 304.

based on outsider ethnicities contributed to the Turkish presence in the region, while also augmenting the South Asian and sub-Saharan African elements. Oman itself actually became a source for Arab manpower recruited by others. Nomadic elements from Iran also appear more frequently, often as raiders.

Trade Routes and Traders

One frequent interpretation of Indian Ocean trade patterns is that, prior to the 900s, Middle Eastern sailors went as far as China and that, afterwards, they only went as far as India or sometimes Southeast Asia. There is, however, no evidence of a major, lasting change in route patterns. There are route books and stories from the ninth century showing Arab and Persian sailors going as far as China, but there is no reason to believe many traders didn't run shorter routes. Similarly, while Abu Zayd al-Srafi's portion of the *Accounts of China and India* and another tenth-century writer named al-Masʿudi mention a halt to voyages to China, this is linked specifically to conditions in China following a revolt which included the massacre of foreign merchants in Guangzhou and more generally the turbulence which followed the fall of the Tang dynasty. For the eleventh century, however, Chinese sources record multiple embassies from Gulf ports to the court of China's Song dynasty. These embassies would have been mainly trade missions headed by prominent traders from the ports in question. Embassies from Sohar came in 1011 and 1072. In 1073, there was an embassy from al-Qatif. We also know of later voyages, such as that of Jamal al-Din al-Tibi, discussed below.[10]

Prominent traders continued to play a role in politics and religion. Ramisht of Siraf, who died in 1140 and whose ships

---

[10] The Chinese sources are discussed in Yajima Hikoichi, "Maritime Activities of the Arab Gulf People and the Indian Ocean World in the Eleventh and Twelfth Centuries," *Journal of Asian and African Studies* 14 (1977), 189–208 at 202–3.

played a role in breaking the Kishite siege of Aden described above, was among the most prominent merchants of his time. His fleet of ships was mentioned in letters from Jewish traders in Yemen, who used it to ship their own goods to India. As a philanthropist he endowed a Sufi lodge in Mecca, where Ramisht himself was buried. His regional prominence allowed him to endow the Kaʿaba itself with a golden waterspout, as well as provide a new cover for it when one was torn. An inscription on his tomb called him the "refuge of the two sanctuaries," which would imply he also financially contributed to Medina.[11]

Another merchant originally from Qalhat named Abu ʿAli became an official at the court of Maʿabar, a kingdom in southeastern India which should not be confused with the subcontinent's southwestern Malabar coast. He was succeeded by his son Sayyid (or Saʿid?), who after Qubilai Khan conquered the Song in the 1270s began setting himself up as a middleman between China and the Ilkhanate, sending ships and envoys regularly in both directions. The ruler of Maʿabar, however, opposed this, and when he fell into some danger, Ibn Abu ʿAli relocated to China in 1291, receiving honours until his death in 1299.[12]

With the shift in trade to the lower Gulf, we also see new caravan routes rising to prominence and, in fact, many new trading families have names such as "Fali" and "Abzari" showing their origin in Iranian trading centres inland. We also see significant caravan trade across Arabia. Although the ʿUqaylids, like previous dynasties in al-Hasa, did not develop as a maritime power, they did revive dormant caravan routes west

---

11 S. M. Stern, "Rāmisht of Sīrāf: A Merchant Millionaire of the Twelfth Century," *Journal of the Royal Asiatic Society of Great Britain and Ireland* no. 1/2 (April 1967), 10–14.

12 Liu Yingsheng, "An Inscription in Memory of Sayyid Bin Abu Ali: A Study of Relations between China and Oman from the Eleventh to the Fifteenth Century," in *The Silk Roads: Highways of Culture and Commerce*, ed. Vadime Elisseeff (New York: Berghahn, 2000), 124–25.

across the desert. Taking advantage of the contemporary boom in Gulf trade, beginning in the 1300s, they travelled annually to Cairo with a caravan of pearls, horses, and goods from the Indian Ocean trade and returned with livestock, fabrics, and sugar.

Finally, as it remained the Indian Ocean port of Mesopotamia, Basra continued as a trading centre, albeit with a smaller volume than before. During the late Middle Ages, accounts of the Basra area show different channels being used for different routes. In the 1200s, ships leaving Basra for India would take a channel by Abadan, while those returning would pass by Dawraqistan, a town and island of Khuzistan with a large population of mariners. During the 1500s, and probably earlier, a western branch around an island in the Shatt al-ʿArab was used by ships headed to al-Hasa and Bahrain, while those headed to Hormuz used the larger channel on the other side.[13]

Horses and Pearls

During this period, horses joined pearls as high value exports from the Persian Gulf. Although the breed of horse known today as Arabian appeared only about two centuries ago, horses have long been significant in Arabian culture. One of the builders of Arab genealogy as described in chapter two also wrote an account and partial genealogy of famous Arabian horses in which he said that horse breeding was begun by the prophet Sulayman (Solomon), son of Dawud (David). Iran also had its own equestrian traditions. It was the birthplace of the game of polo, and in fact the prestige of elite Sasanian cavalry may have led to the animal's adoption as a status symbol in Arabia.[14]

---

13 Verkinderen, *Waterways*, 160, 227–28.

14 Sasanian influence on Arabian horse culture is argued in Nathaniel Miller, "Tribal Poetics in Early Arabic Culture: The Case

The seaborne horse trade between India and Arabia began around 1000, and in India specialized horse merchants traded the animals from the Malabar coast to the Coromandel coast of southeastern India, supplying the latter's Chola rulers and perhaps trading them on across the Bay of Bengal. In India's classification of horses by the place of origin, those brought across the sea from the Middle East were the most valuable, running to between 1000 and 4000 tankas in Ibn Battuta's time. For comparison, the most expensive horses from Central Asia cost 500 tankas, with 100 tankas being a more typical price.[15]

By the 1200s, horses were part of the revived Gulf trade, as well. Demand in India was fuelled by the need for heavy cavalry as the amount and style of warfare shifted in the wake of the establishment of Turkish rule in the subcontinent's north. The Venetian traveller Marco Polo mentioned dealers bringing horses from interior Iran to Kish and Hormuz, while also noting horse traders in Qalhat. He describes the animals as riding on top of the covered cargo on dhows, and both he and a Persian courtier called Wassaf put the number exported each year at about ten thousand. During the 1300s, there is a report of special, large ships just for horses.[16]

India never developed much of its own breeding, and in fact, the horses sent there had short and unpleasant lives. First of all, the environment was not friendly to horses. Beyond that, however, Maʿabar and the other southern Indian polities never developed appropriate horse handling knowl-

---

of *Ashʿār al-Hudhaliyyīn*" (PhD diss., University of Chicago, 2016), 147–58.

15 Ranabir Chakravarti, "Equestrian Demand and Dealers: The Early Indian Scenario (up to c. 1300)," in *Pferde in Asien: Geschichte, Handel und Kultur*, ed. Bert G. Fragner, Ralph Kauz, Roderich Ptak, Angela Schottenhammer (Vienna: Austrian Academy of Sciences Press, 2009), 145–60 at 157–59.

16 Ralph Kauz, "Horse Exports from the Persian Gulf until the Arrival of the Portuguese," in *Pferde in Asien*, ed. Fragner et al. 129–36.

edge. Marco Polo was shocked to see horses being fed cooked food such as boiled rice and meat; Wassaf singled out butter-roasted peas and barley washed down with boiled cow's milk. In addition, they were often tied in their stall for weeks at a time and only taken out to ride when needed, not getting regular exercise. According to Polo, the Gulf merchants tried to keep the Indians ignorant so their horses would keep dying and they would need to buy more.

We know little about the practices of breeding these horses around the Gulf. Although for several hundred years now the region's horse breeding has been matrilineal, evidence indicates it was patrilineal in early Islamic times, and we simply don't know when it changed and how it might have varied regionally. We do know that in addition to Oman and Iran, al-Hasa was known for its horses, and they were frequently sent from there as tribute or as a trade good. The Tibis, whom we will discuss below, bred many of their horses in al-Qatif.[17]

The pearling industry in the Gulf also continued to develop in later medieval times. Its aggressive development may be the reason that prices for individual pearls fell steadily from the early Abbasid period on, though fortunes were still to be made in volume and from exceptional finds. Such fortunes led to an attempted technological innovation as, in the early eleventh century, some divers used a sort of leather diving suit with a long breathing tube leading to the surface, though this seems not to have caught on. By the 1100s, however, sieves were being used for pearling around Bahrain. In the 1240s in Baghdad, most pearls were sold in bunches of strings, with ten strings of thirty-six pearls each being typical.

---

17 Hylke Hettema, "Al-Khamsa: The Prophet's Mares—Or Were They Stallions?" *Cheiron: The International Journal of Equine and Equestrian History* 1 (2021): unpag., doi: 10.22618/TP.Cheiron. 20211.1.233008; Alwazzan, "Politics," 51, 95, 143, 154.

Jamal al-Din al-Tibi

In the late 1200s, Jamal al-Din Ibrahim al-Tibi became perhaps the most successful merchant in the history of the Persian Gulf. His career shows the importance of family networks, the importance of the pearl and horse trades, the fusion of commerce and politics, and the opportunities afforded by the rise of the Mongols. Jamal al-Din was born in 1232 in Baghdad to a family which originally hailed from a village in lower Iraq and traded in simple clay drinking vessels. He, however, became skilled at drilling pearls for jewelry, and became a pearl merchant. During the 1250s, he went to Kish and acquired a huge quantity of pearls for his Baghdad business, which throve.[18]

With the profits from this venture, he and his brother Taqi al-Din Abd al-Rahman then undertook a lengthy Indian Ocean voyage to expand their reach. The two brothers first went to the Swahili coast of Africa, and from there to the southeastern coast of India where the ports had become major emporia between the Arabian Sea and Bay of Bengal. Thereafter they went to China. On the way home they stopped again in southeastern India, where in 1268 Taqi al-Din entered the service of the ruling Pandya dynasty. Jamal al-Din continued on, and settled in Shiraz in Fars, where he became an agent of a merchant named Shams al-Din Taziku al-Yazdi (Gill, 179).

Shams al-Din was an *ortoq* merchant, which as mentioned above means that Mongol royals and government officials provided him with funds to conduct business on their behalf. Jamal al-Din continued to work in pearls, which were particularly valued by the Mongols. During the 1270s, he went with Shams al-Din to the Ilkhans' court and met his employer's patrons, the grand vizier and a prominent military commander, both of whom he impressed enough that they granted him *ortoq*

---

18 The account of Jamal al-Din's career here is from Matanya Gill, "Jamāl al-Dīn al- Ṭībī: The Iraqi Trader Who Traversed Asia" in *Along the Silk Roads in Mongol Eurasia: Generals, Merchants, and Intellectuals*, ed. Michal Biran, Jonathan Z. Brack, and Francesca Fiaschetti (Oakland: University of California Press, 2020), 175–93.

status, as well. With 60,000 dinars from them, he acquired some pearls from Hormuz and made it into jewelry valued at 360,000 dinars. The two patrons offered further generous revenue, and profitable relationship ensued (Gill, 180).

In 1281, Jamal al-Din was contracted to collect the taxes of Fars for the Ilkhans, and in 1293, he became its governor. In these and earlier tax-farming rights he was granted as a way to earn business capital, he gained a reputation for treating the populace fairly, perhaps due to his own lower middle class beginnings. From his base of operations in Kish, he also continued to trade across the Indian Ocean. The same year in which he became Fars's governor, his brother Taqi al-Din became vizier at the Pandya court, and the brothers collaborated to ensure the family business prospered as they claimed the most valuable trade goods for themselves. In addition to pearls, they were now trading horses, with ten thousand allegedly being exported on their ships each year (Gill, 181–82).

For his services to the Ilkhanate, Jamal al-Din had earned from the Ilkhans the title "Malik al-Islam," or "King of Islam." In 1296, however, he earned the contract for tax collection in Iraq and the lease of some lands, but ran into difficulty paying the associated fees, resulting in his being summoned to court two years later. An attempt to recover his fortunes involving an Ilkhanate trade mission to China headed by his son failed, and in 1302 he lost his position on Kish when a rival promised better financial results. Although he was allowed to continue as a trader, his brother's death in 1303 brought an end to that connection. He died in 1306, spending the last year of his life as the fiscal administrator for Shiraz (183–85).

* * *

The Persian Gulf continued to be a prominent conduit for trade throughout the medieval period, although ports, products, and political power shifted along with broader historical forces. At the same time, religious life changed as schools of thought and movements of piety which are now familiar parts of the religion took recognizable shape and were felt throughout the region.

Chapter 5

Islamic Sects in the Late Medieval Gulf

Today, Westerners often associate the Gulf with religious conflict. On one side, Iran promotes a Shi'ite religious ideology, while on the other, Saudi Arabia's official form of Sunni Islam, founded by Muhammad b. Abd al-Wahhab in the 1700s, sees Shi'ites as heretical innovators, and its leaders have often persecuted those in al-Hasa. Bahrain and Iraq have both seen internal conflict between Sunnis and Shi'ites. Contrary to occasional media headlines, these conflicts are in fact over strictly modern issues such as the distribution of national resources, but partisans still seek to martial history in making claims to local prominence and authenticity. Thus, modern Arabian Sunnis often say the Shi'ite population only dates to a period in the 1600s when al-Hasa was part of the Persian Safavid Empire, while Shi'ites in Bahrain and the nearby oases see the population as Shi'ite from the earliest decades of Islam, with Sunnis as later immigrants from central Arabia.

The actual religious history of the Gulf is far more complex. Chapter one described the origins of Islam and the beginnings of its distinct branches, particularly the Shurat, out of which Ibadism developed. Sunnism and Shi'ism were also taking shape by the 700s, but their distinctive elements were not yet developed, and we do not have clear evidence we can associate with them in the Gulf until the period covered in chapter four (trade after 1000). What follows below highlights information about different sectarian movements in the Gulf, occasionally reaching back into the past to explain how they came to be different. It also discusses Sufism, which has its roots partially in Basra and Abadan, but also developed into influential orders, one of which played a role in Gulf commerce.

Shi'ism in the Gulf

Shi'ism comes from the Arabic for a group of followers, indicating here those who believe that ʿAli, Muhammad's cousin and son-in-law, should have succeeded him as leader of the Muslim community. Although ʿAli did have partisans in the early days of Islam, the modern doctrines of Shi'ism took time to develop. The most distinctive is the idea of the imamate, according to which in every generation there is a divinely guided successor to Muhammad from among his descendants through ʿAli. That divinely guided successor is known as the "Imam," the same title used among all Muslims for one who leads prayer. The idea of a Mahdi, a rightly guided messianic leader who would inaugurate a new age of justice, also gained prominence among Shi'ites. Many of the Zutt were Shi'ite in the eighth century, and we see Shi'ite sympathies in funerary inscriptions from Siraf, several of which mention the family of Muhammad, by the 900s.[19]

Shortly after this doctrine of the imamate was established during the mid-700s, a dispute arose over the proper line of the imamate. Each imam was designated by his predecessor, but in one case the person designated, Ismaʿil, seems to have predeceased his father, Jaʿfar. Nonetheless, some argued either that Ismaʿil himself remained alive as a hidden imam, or that the imamate now passed through the line of his son, Muhammad b. Ismaʿil. The most important Ismaʿili movement was that of the Fatimids, a dynasty which claimed descent from Muhammad b. Ismaʿil. Named for Fatima, wife of ʿAli and daughter of the prophet Muhammad, they estab-

---

19 Richardson, *Roma*, 26–27; Nicholas Lowick, *Siraf XV: The Coins and Monumental Inscriptions* (London: The British Institute of Persian Studies, 1985), 92–108.

lished a state in North Africa at the start of the tenth century, several decades before they conquered Egypt, which became their new base.

Both medieval and modern authors often ascribe Ismaʿili beliefs to the Qarmatians, mentioned in the last chapter, who in 899 established a state in eastern Arabia that would last over one hundred and fifty years. However, it is not at all clear that such a description is accurate. A standard account is that they believed that Muhammad b. Ismaʿil was the true imam, that he was in hiding, and that at some point soon he would appear as the Mahdi. However, the original texts which say this are ultimately connected to the Fatimids, who had an interest in presenting the Qarmatians as having abandoned an original movement that culminated in Fatimid rule. In the words of one modern scholar, "The real difficulty in assessing the Qarmati movement in Bahrayn lies in the scarcity of sources bearing witness to their creed."[20]

The Qarmatian state was founded by Abu Saʿid al-Jannabi. Originally from a port town on the Iranian coast, during the 890s he won support from the Bedouin for his preaching, and soon dominated the coastal towns and oases, eventually threatening Basra and establishing his capital at a settlement called Lahsa. He may have been foretelling the coming of a Mahdi in the year 300 of the Islamic calendar, which began in August 912. He was assassinated the following year by an enslaved Slavic eunuch and was succeeded by his oldest son Saʿid as head of a council of his other sons.

The Mahdi preached by Abu Saʿid may or may not have been Muhammad b. Ismaʿil. Some sources say it was a descendant of Muhammad b. al-Hanafiyya, a son of ʿAli

---

20 The quotation is from Wilferd Madelung, "The Fatimids and Qarmaṭīs of Bahrayn," *Medieval Ismaʿili History and Thought*, ed. Farhad Daftary (Cambridge: Cambridge University Press, 1996), 21–73 at 45, while the connections of various sources with Fatimid accounts is an insight of Michael Brett, *The Rise of the Fatimids: The World of the Mediterranean and the Middle East in the Fourth Century of the Hijra, Tenth Century CE* (Leiden: Brill, 2001), 44.

whose mother was of the Hanafi tribe from the region around modern Riyadh. It is notable, however, that eastern Arabia had seen a messianic religious movement just a generation earlier, one led by the ʿAli b. Muhammad who went on to lead the Zanj revolt discussed in chapter two. What's more, both the Zanj rebels and the Qarmatians criticized the Abbasid elites for their luxurious and sinful lifestyle, showing the persistence of such ideas from the Shurat onward.

Saʿid was quickly eclipsed by his brother Abu Tahir, and during his time the Qarmatians continued to focus on a coming Imam–Mahdi. Based on astrological calculations, many had been expecting the Mahdi in 928, and that year Abu Tahir abruptly ended a military campaign in Iraq to return home, where he built a structure of some sort for those who would travel to al-Hasa to enter the Mahdi's service. In a fragment of poetry which survives, Abu Tahir claims he will live until the second coming of ʿIssa (Jesus), who is involved in Islamic eschatology. In 930, the Qarmatians even seized the Black Stone of the Kaʿba, the focus of pilgrimage to Mecca, probably to symbolize their expected new dispensation.[21]

In 931, Abu Tahir actually proclaimed that a young Persian prisoner known only as "The Isfahani" after an Iranian city was the expected Mahdi. Whether this was from sincere belief or political calculation is impossible to know. This newly proclaimed messiah proceeded to declare all religions invalid, various former sins now acceptable, and ordered the execution of several Qarmatian leaders. After eighty days, Abu Tahir announced that he had made a mistake and had the youth killed. Many of the Qarmatian leader's followers then left, though he continued to dominate the state, which survived for well over a century more.[22]

---

21 Madelung, "The Fatimids," 48–49.

22 Hajnal, "Some Aspects," 235–36.

In 1051, the Persian traveller named Nasir-i Khusraw passed through al-Hasa.[23] He reported that the people there did not pray or fast and called themselves Busaʿidis after Abu Saʿid, whom they believed would return from the dead. Abu Saʿid had reportedly told his sons that the way to recognize him upon his return was to strike his neck with a sword, and if he immediately returned to life, then it was him. His tomb was a prominent shrine in the city, and there was a continual watch for his resurrection and a horse kept ready for him. The six sayyids had a palace and ruled consultatively, much the way the system theoretically worked under Saʿid and Abu Tahir. A Persian who had performed the pilgrimage to Mecca paid for a mosque used by pilgrims in Lahsa. Islamic dietary law also seems to have been in abeyance, as the Qarmatians raised cats and dogs for food despite the fact Muslims cannot generally eat the meat of carnivores.

As described by Nasir-i Khusraw, the Qarmatians had a distributive state where the peasants were not taxed, and were in fact supported if they fell into debt or had damage to their property beyond their ability to repair. Craftsmen were given start-up loans, and people could have their wheat ground for free at mills maintained by the sayyids. A currency of wrapped lead tokens was used internally. The wealth distributed came not only from tribute payments, but from the 50 percent tax taken by the rulers on Bahrain's pearl harvest. Those rulers also may have owned most of the fields and date orchards worked by thousands of Ethiopian and Zanj slaves.

In contrast to the Ismaʿilis, the Twelver Shi'ites followed a different line of imams involving another son of Jaʿfar and brother of Ismaʿil. Their name comes from the fact that the twelfth in this line, Muhammad al-Mahdi, disappeared as a child in 874, but is believed to still be alive as the Hidden Imam who would one day return as the Mahdi. Twelver Shi'ism was particularly promoted by the Buyids, the Daylamite dynasty

---

23 All this paragraph and the next are from Nasir-i Khusraw, *Book of Travels*, ed. Thackston, 112–14.

in Iraq and Iran, beginning in the late 900s, though multiple forms of Islam were practised in their domains, and they in fact accepted honours from and ruled in the name of the Abbasid caliphs.

The earliest evidence of Twelver Shi'ism in Bahrain comes from the period of the ʿUyunids. The twelve imams are mentioned in an inscription from 1124–1125 on one of the two minarets of al-Khamis Mosque in the medieval Bahraini capital of Bilad al-Qadim. This inscription was ordered by an otherwise unknown Maʾali b. al-Hasan b. ʿAli b. Hammad, who took credit in it for building either the minaret or the mosque itself. The same minaret, however, has another inscription from the ʿUyunid emir at the time in which he claims the title of "al-Qaʾim," another term for the Mahdi which was important in Ismaʾili circles. Scholars have seen that ʿAlid shrines in Syria during this period were patronized by people with multiple religious perspectives, and the same is probably true here, with an ʿUyunid messianic title similar to those seen in the region for centuries coexisting with an expression of Twelver Shi'ism.[24]

By the 1300s, it would seem Bahrain was predominantly Twelver. At that time, Hamd Allah Mustawfi, a Twelver Shi'ite Persian writer, described its people as proper Muslims, exempting only those who practised raiding at sea. Twelver beliefs are evidenced by a seal bearing the names of the twelve imams from the merchants' quarter of the island's main settlement at the time. From the same site we also have prayer stones which Shi'ites pressed against their head during prayer prostrations. They were made of clay from near a holy place, and in this case they were from Mashhad, a site in northeastern Iran where the eighth imam was buried. They were also etched with the imams' names.[25]

---

24 On Syria, see Stephennie Mulder, *The Shrines of the ʿAlids in Medieval Syria: Sunnis, Shi'is, and the Architecture of Coexistence* (Edinburgh: Edinburgh University Press, 2014).

25 On the archaeological remains, see Venetia Porter, "Arabic

Twelver Shi'ism spread elsewhere, and in 1310 the Mongol Ilkhan Uljeitu himself converted, promoting it for the remaining six years of his life. Understanding the patterns of its spread, however, is challenging, as we can see in the case of Basra. A writer from the late tenth century said that its people were Shi'ites, though he did not specify what imam they believed in. Mustawfi declared that its people were Shi'ites, but his contemporary Ibn Battuta, a Moroccan traveller who went as far as China and Mali, said it was a Sunni city. Most likely the population remained mixed, united mainly by their set of common Muslim holy figures as we will describe below.

Sunnism and Ibadism

The name for Sunni Islam comes from the Arabic phrase *Ahl al-Sunna wa-al-Jami'a*, meaning "People of tradition and community." The "tradition" (*sunna*) here meant the accounts maintained of Muhammad's practices as known via hadith. Its underlying supposition might be that, in contrast to the Shi'ite belief that the community had strayed by not following the imams, Muslims as a whole had gotten things right. Although the caliphs could serve as symbols of unity and authorize secular powers, there was no higher religious authority than the scholars who had studied the Qur'an and hadith in the process of articulating doctrine and building up Islamic jurisprudence.

The Seljuq Turks aggressively promoted Sunni Islam during their rule, and the Gulf region was no exception, as it saw the foundation of schools for training Sunni religious scholars. This is not to say that there was no coexistence with other forms of Islam. In fact, during this period Sunni Islam was still in a state of flux as religious scholars and others developed their ideas about what would be in and out of their new consensus and the boundaries of belief. As a sign of this

Inscriptions from Qala'at al-Bahrain Excavations," in *Islamic Remains in Bahrain*, ed. Karen Frifelt (Aarhus: Moesgaard Museum / Aarhus University Press, 2001), 201–2.

coexistence, we can look at the second minaret of Bahrain's al-Khamis Mosque, which we mentioned above. This minaret was erected in 1324 at the orders of one calling himself "reviver of jihad," which is usually a Sunni claim but is found coexisting on the same mosque that had the Shi'ite inscriptions.[26]

Sunni jurisprudence developed several different schools of thought, and all four which still exist today were present in the medieval Gulf. One, the Shafi'is, comes from a ninth-century scholar who developed a rigid intellectual system of using the Qur'an and hadith, followed by analogy if a situation was not clearly addressed in this, and finally the consensus of religious scholars if necessary. The Hanafis used the same sources as the Shafi'is, but also allow for the use of local custom and juristic discretion. This was and is the most common school of thought in the Islamic world as a whole. The Hanbalis, on the other hand, accept only the Qur'an and hadith, as well as, if necessary, views from the first generation of Muslims. They allow for analogy only as a last resort. Today this is the dominant school of thought in much of the Arabian Peninsula. Finally, the Malikis, who today are found mainly in north and west Africa, privilege the practices of Medina, as that city's Muslim community was most influenced by Muhammad in his lifetime.

Understanding the history of these schools of thought in the Gulf region is tricky in that we find information indicating their presence, but tracking their influence over time is difficult. It is clear that all four of these schools of thought were present in Basra, which as one of the first truly Muslim cities had a long tradition of Islamic religious learning. Regarding other areas, however, the accounts from al-Hasa are typical. In the 1050s, the Qarmatians were deposed by an emir who professed the Hanafi branch of Islamic law. In the early 1300s, some villagers from eastern Arabia sent a delegation to Egypt seeking opinions on certain religious matters from

---

26 The inscription quotation is from Alwazzan, "Politics," 144–45.

Ibn Taymiyya, a controversial Hanbali religious scholar. However, we cannot say that that the Hanafis did not last into the 1300s or that the Hanbalis were a new community.

The Shafi'is were, it seems, the most prominent Sunni school of jurisprudence in the Gulf. This school of thought dominated much of Iran and was promoted by the Salghurids. In India, the Malabar coast's Muslim community had many families whose ancestors came from the Red Sea and Persian Gulf regions, and they brought Shafi'ism there as well.[27] One example of how jurisprudential schools might matter is seen with regard to family law. For example, according to the Shafi'is, only the father or grandfather of a minor can serve as that minor's consenting guardian in a marriage, whereas other schools could allow brothers, uncles, or nephews. The Hanafis do not require any consenting guardian for the marriage of a female minor; they also allow the husband much greater freedom to divorce.

During this period, Oman, too, saw a flourishing of Sunni Islam. The Ibadi imamate collapsed amidst a civil war at the end of the 800s, and the country entered a period of control by the Buyids, Seljuqs, and their local Omani allies. Many in northern Oman adopted Shafi'ism, alienated by the tribal backers of one of the parties related to the civil war. Sohar also had schools for both the Hanafi and Hanbali doctrines, and during the twelfth and thirteenth centuries people came from around the Gulf to study there. The country even had a presence of the now defunct Zahiri school of thought, which like the Hanbalis worked from only the Qur'an and hadith.[28]

It is in this context that, by the twelfth century, Ibadism had come more and more to resemble Sunnism. The term

---

27 On Shafi'is in Malabar, see Stephen Dale, *Islamic Society on the South Asian Frontier: The Māpillas of Malabar, 1498–1922* (Oxford: Clarendon, 1980), 26.

28 Wilkinson, *Ibâḍism*, 422–23; Valeria Fiorani Piacentini, "Merchant Families in the Gulf—A Mercantile and Cosmopolitan Dimension: The Written Evidence," *ARAM Periodical* 11, no. 1 (1999), 145–59 at 152–53.

sunna, for example, came to be used only in the sense used by Sunnis, as the practice of Muhammad witnessed by traditions about him, whereas before it could also refer to practices of the righteous Muslim community. Also like Sunnis, and for that matter Shi'ites, this *sunna* was known through hadith. Earlier Ibadis had privileged the consensus of their religious scholars, but as that consensus increasingly involved determinations made on hadith, those accounts were filtered into Ibadism. Ibadis even began to describe their tradition of learning as a *madhhab*, noted above as the term for a Sunni school of thought, and became similar in method to the Shafi'is.

Oman in the early 1100s came under the rule of the Banu Nabhan, who dominated most of the country for the next five centuries. However, in tandem with the spread of Sunnism in that region, they did not rule in the name of Ibadism, and used the Seljuq title of "sultan" rather than call themselves "imams." Because of this, they were not considered important by later chroniclers concerned primarily with the Ibadi community and its leadership, and so we know little about them. One window into their early decades comes from a panegyric poet named Ahmad b. Sa'id al-Satali. From his works, it appears that at that time different Nabhani leaders ruled different cities of Oman's interior and they also maintained contact with Africa's Swahili coast. The fact some of his poems begin by praising the wine at feasts shows their lack of interest in religious credentials.[29]

Ibadism in the Gulf was not limited to Oman, though information about it elsewhere is scarce. By the tenth century, Ibadis predominated in the coastal towns of Makran, as they did in the 1100s on the island of Qeshm, which had historically been close to Oman. There were also some in Basra and

---

29 Hasan M. al-Naboodah, "Banū Nabhān in the Omani Sources," in *New Arabian Studies, 4*, ed. G. Rex Smith, J. R. Smart, and B.R. Pridham (Exeter: Exeter University Press, 1997), 181–89.

al-Hasa and/or Bahrain in the 1200s.[30] Again, however, the religious history of these areas is very unclear.

Sufism

Sufism, put simply, is Islamic mysticism, a movement seeking personal emotional experience of the divine beyond the forms of worship and obedience to Islamic precepts. Although the term is used for a blending of several strands of thought and practice, one, asceticism, became important in early Islamic Basra. The city had the two most famous eighth-century Muslim ascetics in Hasan al-Basri (d. 728) and Rabiʿa al-ʿAdawiyya (d. 801), though the life of both is shrouded in pious legend. Both seem to have come from low social backgrounds and to have attracted circles of followers. In sermons, Hasan warned of the Last Judgment and the need to always be prepared for it, while Rabiʿa focused on God as an object of all-encompassing love for his own sake and even lamented the idea that some might follow him only from concern with the afterlife.

It was in Abadan that the first Sufi retreat was developed during the mid-700s. It may have been founded by some of Hasan al-Basri's disciples, though it may also have grown out of a military garrison guarding against Indian pirates, a garrison whose internal culture involved ascetic religious devotion. One ascetic who spent time at Abadan during the 800s was Sahl al-Tustari, who later settled in Basra. He taught that constant recollection of God, such as by repetition of a divine name, led to a closer relationship with him, a core practice of later Sufism.

For centuries, Abadan remained home to Sufi lodges, while also developing a shrine to al-Khidr, a mysterious figure from the Qur'an who assists those in need and was sometimes combined with the prophet Elijah. Offerings from seafarers and pilgrims were crucial for the economy, while the

---

30 Abdulrahman Al-Salimi, *Ibāḍism East of Mesopotamia: Early Islamic Iran, Central Asia, and India* (Berlin: Schwartz, 2016), 160–61.

Sufis also fished. The city also served as an emporium for goods from Basra. In terms of famous local products, people made mats from the local wetland reeds. These mats were sold across the Muslim world and imitated in both Iran and Egypt.

By the 1100s, Sufism throughout the Muslim world was becoming organized into orders. Each order traced itself back to a founding mystic and was characterized by a distinct set of practices. The orders had their own lodges, and a hierarchical relationship existed in which masters instructed the disciples. Most people in the cities maintained some attachment to Sufi orders, and mystics were widely venerated much as we saw Christian monks venerated in chapter one. Even the rulers and other wealthy people would bestow wealth upon favoured holy men: The prominent merchant and governor Jamal al-Din Tibi provided annual support to a favoured mystic from Baghdad and settled his debts after his death.[31] Many of these holy figures were also believed to have performed miracles.

The Kazeruni Sufi order was particularly important, not only in the Gulf, but the wider Indian Ocean region. It was named for the city of Kazerun, about 150 km inland from the northeast part of the Gulf, along the caravan route between Bushehr and Shiraz and a prominent staging area for goods. Its founder, Abu Ishaq, was born in 963 to parents who had converted to Islam from Zoroastrianism. At the age of fifteen he began following the Sufi path, and some time later began preaching in front of a prominent mosque. During this period, Kazerun was the site of conflict between Muslims and Zoroastrians, and the latter sought to interfere with his preaching. As a new quarter of the city developed around a mosque he had constructed himself, this conflict escalated into violent clashes which were resolved by the Buyid vizier in Shiraz.

---

31 For Jamāl al-Dīn al-Ṭībī and the mystic, see Gill, "Jamāl al-Dīn al-Ṭībī," 182–83.

Abu Ishaq died in 1033, but his reputation as a holy man spread, carried along the commercial routes from his native city. By the 1300s, people had come to believe that he could protect ships at sea, and so when a danger at sea arose, they would pledge a portion of their wealth to the saint if they came through it safely. Kazeruni lodges were found all around the Indian Ocean, and when a ship docked, votaries from the lodge would board the ship to take possession of what had been pledged.[32]

Christians and Jews

Benjamin of Tudela, a Jewish traveller from Spain who passed through the Gulf on his travels between 1165 and 1173, provides an unusual witness to the Jewish communities of the twelfth century. He reports a population of ten thousand Jews in Basra, including many scholars and wealthy men, much as we saw in earlier centuries. He also visited what many devotees today still consider the tomb of the Biblical Ezra along the Tigris river near the city, where lived another fifteen hundred Jews and which was a joint holy site between Jews and Muslims. Al-Qatif had five thousand Jews, including the man who supervised the pearl fishery on behalf of the ʿUyunids, a remarkable continuation of the Jewish communities mentioned in the early Arabic sources. Kish, however, counted only five hundred Jews.

Christian communities also continued in the Gulf region, though in the tenth century the traveller al-Muqaddasi noted that they were far less numerous than the Jews in the Arabian Peninsula, and Marco Polo did not mention any in thirteenth-century Hormuz, though some were doubtless among the trading community, as they were in later times. Basra, however, continued to have its bishopric. In the early 1200s,

---

32 These two paragraphs are from Ralph Kauz, "A Kazaruni Network," in *Aspects of the Maritime Silk Road: From the Persian Gulf to the East China Sea*, ed. Ralph Kauz (Wiesbaden: Harrassowitz, 2010), 61–69.

Bishop Shlemon of Basra was a prolific author, most famous for *The Book of the Bee*. Its purpose was to show the role of God's will in history, and the name came from the idea that in writing the author had gathered insights the way a bee gathers nectar.[33]

Holy Figures and the Miraculous

A focus on doctrine and formal identity can obscure the fact that, as in previous centuries, most people connected with their religious identity via individuals with an aura of sanctity, found confirmation in the power of miracles, and lived in a landscape studded with sites associated with both. Mustawfi's geography mentioned above frequently highlights the tombs of past figures. For Basra, for example, he mentions several associates of Muhammad whose burial sites were sites of pilgrimage, as well as that of the above-mentioned proto-Sufi Hasan al-Basri, hadith scholars, and others. He also reported that a minaret at Basra's main mosque would quiver to indicate the truth of a statement made under oath to ʿAli b. Abu Talib.

Even religious scholars themselves would be drawn to the charisma of holy figures, and Ibn Battuta regularly sought them out. Under the Ilkhanate the region at the head of the Gulf was the site of frequent conflict and perhaps plague, and Basra moved nearer to the old site of al-Ubulla, where it is still centred today. Both were significantly inland as the shoreline moved further south. As a result, many graves of early Islamic figures were away from the main settlement, and one was even singled out as dangerous to visit alone because of its isolation. Some others, however, offered hospitality to travellers. At the riverside grave of Sahl al-Tustari, Ibn Bat-

---

33 Jonathan A. Loopstra, "Shlemon of Baṣra," in *Shlemon of Baṣra*, ed. Sebastian P. Brock, Aaron M. Butts, George A. Kiraz and Lucas Van Rompay (Piscataway: Gorgias, 2011; in *Gorgias Encyclopedic Dictionary of the Syriac Heritage*, ed. Beth Mardutho, 2018, https://gedsh.bethmardutho.org/Shlemon-of-Basra).

tuta saw sailors drinking the water by it while praying. He also found the lodge dedicated to al-Khidr and Elijah, which had only four devotees and their children. They told him of an Abadan hermit who came to the shore to fish once a month. Ibn Battuta sought him out and found him in a mostly ruined mosque. The hermit blessed him that he might achieve his desire in both this life and the next, and in his account Ibn Battuta said he had the done the former by being able to travel as much as he had.

Around 1200, we have the earliest reports of another shrine, on Kharg. This was a mausoleum of Muhammad b. al-Hanafiyya, one of several claimants to be that son of ʿAli's burial site in different regions. It was important to sea-farers passing by and may have supplanted some sort of older shrine. By this time, a legend had developed in Iran and India that Ibn al-Hanafiyya had avenged his half-brother al-Husayn, whose martyrdom at the hands of the Umayyads is commemorated in the most important distinctively Shi'ite holy day. The present building includes an inscription calling Ibn al-Hanafiiya "Commander of the Believers," a claim to his leadership of the Muslim community which fits with no lasting Shi'ite sect. That same inscription is dated to either 1339 or 1340 and claimed by a Husayn al-Bukhari, perhaps a promi-nent trader or official for a dynasty ruling Kharg.[34]

* * *

---

34 Although the volume on Kharg's archaeology in the Further Reading section includes this shrine, crucial information also comes from Jean Calmard, "Mohammad b. al-Hanafiyya dans la religion populaire, le folklore, les légendes dans le monde turco-persan et indo-persan," *Cahiers d'Asie centrale* 5–6 (1998): 201–20 at 207–11.

Although there were still people of different religions, much of the Persian Gulf had become Muslim by the 1000s. As the centuries passed, that Islam came to include the Twelver Shi'ism, Sunnism with its different schools of jurisprudence, and Ibadism which are familiar today. However, charismatic holy figures, often linked with Sufism, continued to attract devotion as people chose to God whose blessings could bring health, prosperity, merit towards the afterlife, and protection from evil.

Chapter 6

Hormuz

During the fifteenth century, Hormuz was the hegemon of the Persian Gulf. Located on the island of Jarun in what today is called the Strait of Hormuz, it controlled all traffic in and out of this body of water, much as today the strait represents a major choke point in global oil shipping. When in the early 1400s one of China's Ming rulers sent admiral Zheng He with treasure fleets to display his empire's greatness around the Indian Ocean and South China Sea, they stopped at Hormuz, and a Chinese Muslim writer who accompanied the fleets wrote of it glowingly. In the early 1500s, the Portuguese would capture the city and make vassals of its rulers as part of attempting to establish their own dominance, not only in the Gulf, but around the Indian Ocean.[1]

As we have seen in previous chapters, the Hormuz visited and written about by these travellers from opposite ends of Eurasia was but the latest power to control the Gulf's waters. The Hormuzi era, however, is convenient as a window to show the persistence of many of the themes discussed previously

---

1 In addition to the book by Valeria Piacentini Fiorani and the long article by Jean Aubin, two other items listed in Further Reading have crucial material on Hormuz. They are *The Ports of Oman*, which has a long and evocative chapter on it written under the name Valeria Fiorani Piacentini, as well as *The Persian Gulf in History*, with chapters by the eminent Iranian historian Mohammad Bagher Vosoughi and João Teles e Cunha.

in this book, as we have ample testimony to the polity having a society where different religious and ethnic groups mingled together, sometimes with tensions, at other times with conviviality, all while participating in the long-standing livelihoods of the region.

Rise of Hormuz

The original city of Hormuz was not on the island which bears its name today. It was instead a port on the mainland near Minab oasis around 100 km east of modern Bandar Abbas. It first appears as noteworthy in the tenth century as the sea outlet of Kirman and the site of a leading indigo market. Its population grew with an influx of Omani refugees fleeing the conflicts of that country's tenth century, and those ties would crucially shape its later history. Like most of the Iranian shore it had a backdrop of high mountains, and a three-kilometre canal linked it to the sea. During the eleventh and early twelfth centuries, it blossomed under the Seljuq administration described in chapter four.

The first major figure in building Hormuz to its place of supremacy was Mahmud al-Qalhati. A prominent trader, he came to the throne in 1242 via his wife, the daughter of the ruler of Hormuz who had allied with the Salghurids against Kish. He established Hormuz's independence from the continental military forces by growing the navy in alliance with the nearby coast and recruiting manpower from Oman. As part of creating a new system of connections to support Hormuzi power and independence, he also paid attention to defensive fortifications at the various smaller ports, seeing that they were defended from both naval attack and raids from nomads in their hinterland. He further supported their commerce by building new markets and warehouses.

The move to Jarun was the work of Ayaz, who bore the *laqab* honorific of Baha al-Din. Ayaz was originally a Turkish slave of Mahmud al-Qalhati. He may also have been the tutor of Mahmud's son, and that son appointed him governor of the city of Qalhat. When that son was killed by one of his brothers, Ayaz rose against him and seized the throne. As the old site of Hormuz was threatened by nomadic raiders, in 1300 he ordered a move to nearby Qeshm, and then to Jarun, which he acquired from Jamal al-Din al-Tibi. Jarun became known as "New Hormuz," whereas the original site continued as "Old Hormuz." Alongside the new settlement, however, Ayaz continued to regularly visit Qalhat, which became effectively a second capital.

As another example of the variety of cultural influences in Gulf history, the Mongols inspired greater political roles for women during this period. This influence becomes most visible in the career of Baha al-Din Ayaz's wife, Bibi Maryam. In the steppes, Mongol women had enabled a greater share of the men to engage in combat by managing camps, including rear camps serving support functions during campaigns, while also having advisory roles in leadership decisions. This continued into political roles in the Mongol empire and its offshoots. In chapter four we saw Salghurid women as nominal rulers. Mahmud al-Qalhati's wife also seems to have deliberately engineered his rise to the throne by marrying him and then orchestrating the assassination of the current ruler, while in the 1300s women appear as mediators between factions within Hormuz's politics.[2]

During the reign of Baha al-Din Ayaz, Bibi Maryam served as governor of Qalhat in his absence. To her is credited the Mausoleum of Bibi Maryam, which today is the last remaining building from medieval Qalhat, and which may have been the burial place of Baha al-Din himself. She continued to rule in Qalhat after her husband's death, and in yet another of Hormuz's succession disputes, sheltered two brothers who became the ultimate victors. One of those brothers then took the throne as Qutb al-Din Tahamtan II, and it was he who brought Hormuz to dominance in the Gulf and whom later generations regarded as the kingdom's true founder.

---

2 This background to the political prominence of Mongol women is from Anne Broadbridge, *Women and the Making of the Mongol Empire* (Cambridge: Cambridge University Press, 2018).

Figure 2. Bibi Maryam's Mausoleum in Qalhat, Oman.
Photograph by Richard Mortel. Used with permission.

Qutb al-Din Tahamtan II earned this reputation by finally defeating Kish, which at that time still dominated the Gulf trade, but which Hormuz's control of the entrance to the Gulf threatened. Shortly after his accession, the ruler of Kish, a grandson of Jamal al-Din Ibrahim al-Tibi, sought to seize Jarun while Qutb al-Din was at the original mainland Hormuz. Qutb al-Din, however, quickly moved against Kish, and in 1332–1333 took the island and deported all Jamal al-Din's children and grandchildren who were there. Shortly thereafter, he was recognized by the Ilkhan Abu Saʿid as the ruler of all the shores of the Gulf, with sources singling out Bahrain and al-Hasa as areas of interest. Perhaps because of the importance of Bahrain's pearls, he installed his nephews there as governors.

Hormuz at its Height

The island of Jarun, as it was then known, is eighteen kilometres in diameter with two natural bays on its east and west, but close enough together for them to be treated as one. Next to this was a sandy strip where the city was built. Behind the city, hills rose sharply. By the sea were the royal palace and bazaar, and on narrow streets behind them were houses made of the island's light stone and coral from the sea. Behind this residential district were mansions and mosques. The island had a few springs, one of which was in the 1500s exclusively for the king. Their brackish water was mostly used for irrigation. Water was imported daily from Qeshm and Larak, and access to the cisterns was rationed.

Because of the different colours of its stone and earth, the island stood out to travellers for its panoply of colours. According to Ma Huan, who travelled with the fleets of Zheng He, it was "a great mountain of colors different on each of the four sides...green as rock salt, white as gypsum, red as blood, and yellow as clay." Today the "Rainbow Valley" is still noted as an attraction in tourist publications. The different coloured salt was also used locally to make tableware and lamp pedestals, and Fei Xin, another Chinese traveller with Zheng He noted that the salt from the dishes rubbed off onto the food, which as a result was always salty.[3]

The reign of Turanshah II from 1436 until 1470 may represent Hormuz's cultural and economic apogee. In 1442, Shah Rukh, ruler of Iran and much of Central Asia, sent an ambassador to a ruler from India's Malabar Coast. That ambassador, Abd al-Razzaq al-Samarqandi, went by way of Hormuz, and described the city thus:

"Hormuz...is a port in the midst of the sea with no equal on the face of the earth. Merchants from the seven climes—Egypt, Syria, Anatolia, Azerbaijan, Arabian and Persian Iraq, Fars, Khurasan, Transoxiana, Turkistan, the Qipchaq Steppe, the Qalmaq regions, and all the lands of the Orient, China, and Khan-Baliq—all come to that port, and seafaring men, from Indo-China, Java, Bengal Ceylon, the cities of Zirbad (Malaysia), Tennaserim, Sumatra, Siam, and the Maldive Islands to the realm of Malibar, Abyssinia and Zanzibar, the

3 Information on accounts of Hormuz from Zheng He's expeditions is from Ralph Kauz and Roderich Ptak, "Hormuz in Yuan and Ming Sources," *Bulletin de l'École française d'Extrême-Orient* 88 (2001): 27–75.

ports of Vijayanagar Gulbarga, Gujarat, and Cambay, the coast of the Arabian peninsula to Aden, Jiddah and the Yanbu bring to that town precious and rare commodities which are made glittering by the sun, moon, and clouds and which can be transported across the sea. Travelers from everywhere in the world come there, and everything they bring for exchange for what they want can be found without much search in that town. They deal both in cash and in barter, and the *divanis* take a tenth of everything except gold and silver. Adherents of various religious, even infidels, are many in that city, but they deal equitably with all. For this reason, the town is called Dar al-Aman (Abode of Security)."[4]

One modern scholar has highlighted that Hormuz was not divided into quarters, and that people of different religions and ethnicities all mingled together both residentially and commercially. The population included Arabs and Persians, people from South Asia and eastern Africa, and probably others, such as smaller ethnicities from Iran or those from further away. Despite claims by Ma Huan that there were no poor in Hormuz, however, there was a division among social classes and occupations clustered along certain streets. A portion of the working class split time between shipping-related work on the island and harvesting dates on the mainland, and much of the population left for cooler environments during the heat of summer.[5]

Mention should also be made of Qalhat, the realm's second capital. Qalhat was a triangular city wedged between the mountains and the sea on the bank of a stream in a valley leading into the Gulf of Oman. Buildings were found along straight streets or around city squares, and a wide area with-

---

4 "Kamaluddin Abdul-Razzaq Samarqandi: Mission to Calicut and Vijayanagar," in *A Century of Princes: Sources on Timurid History and Art*, ed. and trans. W. M. Thackston (Cambridge, MA: The Aga Khan Program for Islamic Architecture, 1989), 300.

5 On the mobility of Hormuz's population, see Willem Floor, *The Persian Gulf: A Political and Economic History of Five Port Cities, 1500–1730* (Washington, DC: Mage, 2006), 17.

out architectural remains may have once had the reed huts common to the Gulf's lower classes. Bibi Maryam had constructed a large blue-tiled mosque by the shore. The traveller Ibn Battuta spoke glowingly of its fish, which were boiled on leaves and eaten on a bed of rice. He also noted that, as a colloquialism, the people of the town continually ended sentences with the word "no." Although it remained important when the Portuguese arrived, and its urban pride was undiminished, over the 1400s it was gradually displaced by Muscat., which was much closer to Hormuz.[6]

Hormuz's Trade

As Tamerlane's empire declined, various powers competed for control of the head of the Gulf. These included various Turkmen confederations, as well as the Mushaʿshaʿiyya, a religious group whose first leader claimed to be the Shiʿite Mahdi. At the end of the 1400s, Basra would be a small city under the control of a Bedouin tribe called the Muntafiq. The city served as another Gulf trade hub, fulfilling its longstanding role of connecting the Gulf and Mesopotamia. The modern city of Bushehr had also arisen as a port serving Iran. It is uncertain who ruled al-Hasa until the mid-1400s, when the Jabrids, a branch of the ʿUqyalids, took power. They allied with Hormuz in exchange for control of Bahrain.

Hormuz's control of the Gulf also meant control of its distinctive products: pearls and horses. Ibn Battuta's information on pearling is vague, as he seems to meld together several different areas of the Gulf in his description, but he does mention Arabs of a particular tribe as the divers. These divers were in debt to merchants who funded their dives, and after a fifth of the catch had been taken for the ruler, the

6 The main accounts of Qalhat for this chapter are Axelle Rougeulle, "Medieval Qalhāt, historical *vs* archaeological data," *Arabian Humanities* 9 (2017): unpag., https://doi.org/10.4000/cy.3442 and Tom Vosmer, "Qalhat and Sur," in *The Ports of Oman*, ed. Al Salimi and Staples, 117–38.

merchants took the rest in furtherance of their debts. The system of debt bondage described recurred periodically in the history of pearling in the Gulf, and typifies the conditions found even in the nineteenth and twentieth centuries.

The city of Hormuz itself became the Gulf's main pearl market, though as had often been the case many Gulf pearls were also traded in Baghdad. In 1507, Hormuz actually had a street dedicated to pearl merchants, who displayed their wares on red cloths. As an indicator of how cosmopolitan its trading community was, many of those who traded Gulf pearls in India were from Venice. Pearls were also among the gifts which Hormuz's rulers sent to China's emperors. By the start of the 1500s, Hormuz's rulers had turned the pearling cut into a tax farm.

The horse trade also continued under Hormuz, and horses were a regular part of the tribute on trade missions to China. In his account al-Samarqandi complained about the smell of horses on board his ship; they might have been part of almost every sea voyage. The numbers were down, however, as upon their conquest the Portuguese estimated that around one thousand per year were shipped to India. Qalhat was probably still crucial to the trade; horses there were brought from the coastal plain across the mountains and down the valley of the city's stream. Hormuz was also a transit point for mercenaries, as southern Indian states recruited for their armies.

Hormuz's commercial prosperity depended on having security from stronger great powers and few if any enemies. From around 1300 on we have Hormuzi coins, but they seldom make a political statement by mentioning any rulers.[7] Hormuz's rulers also agreed to pay taxes to larger kingdoms as a means of ensuring security for their realm. Qutb al-Din Tahamtan II, for example, recognized as his overlord the Ilkhan Abu Saʿid, though when that ruler died and the Ilkhanate fell apart, he stopped paying anyone. His succes-

---

7 Hormuzi coinage is described in Kauz and Ptak, "Hormuz," 58.

sors would resume paying taxes on different parts of their domain to rulers of Fars (for the upper Gulf) and Kirman (for the lower). When Tamerlane conquered Iran Hormuz's kings again paid tax revenue to him and his descendants during the 1400s while continuing to rule autonomously.

Ibn Majid and Maritime Knowledge

The continuation of the tradition of maritime knowledge can be seen in the works of Ahmad b. Majid, a pilot of Bedouin descent who lived in the 1400s. He was most active around Oman and may have been from Julfar. Although often said to be the Portuguese Vasco da Gama's navigator through the Indian Ocean, that was actually a Muslim from the state of Gujarat in northwestern India. In describing the significance of the art of navigation, which he traces back to Noah, Ibn Majid calls it "the most difficult thing next to service for kings," the reason being that there can often be no time to correct mistakes before wealth and livelihoods are lost. He also notes that its techniques could also be used to determine the direction of Mecca for Muslim prayer (Tibbetts, 67).[8]

Ibn Majid displays a humility focused on the idea that his is an ever-evolving practical science rather than one in which he could claim to be the ultimate authority. He describes how in earlier days seafarers had much courage and prepared ships well, but there are continually new innovations and new knowledge gained, creating an ever-evolving body of experience. After describing three important predecessors, he says, "I honour them when I say 'I am the fourth of them,' because they only preceded me in time, and after my death men will come who will know the correct place for every one of us" (Tibbetts, 72–73).

---

8 Parenthetical references are to G. R. Tibbetts, *Arab Navigation in the Indian Ocean Before the Coming of the Portuguese* (London: Royal Asiatic Society of Great Britain and Ireland, 1971).

Religion in Hormuz

During the mid-1500s, a Jesuit priest, who was not a fan of the religious diversity he described, acknowledged that in Hormuz God was celebrated four days of the week. Those from India held their devotions on Monday, Muslims on Friday, Jews on Saturday, and Christians on Sunday. The same would have been true in the fifteenth century, as members of all these religious groups were present when the Portuguese arrived. Although some could try to keep their own flocks in line while looking at others' practices with disapproval, the general environment remained one of mutual tolerance. Thus, cattle roamed the streets and were given water by the Hindus, while prayer to the God of Abraham took many forms.

Hormuz's rulers were Sunnis, and Qutb al-Din Tahamtan II had founded a school for training religious scholars on the island. We also have an inscription from al-Qatif proclaiming that ruler's building of a local mosque in which he is called "lord" and "religious scholar," as well as "sultan of land and sea."[9] A real or claimed interest in religious scholarship would become common among the ruling family, several of whom had a reputation for piety. In terms of jurisprudence, most of Hormuz's Sunnis were Shafi'is, as one would expect.

Alongside its Sunni majority, Hormuz had a large community of Shi'ites. Among them were members of the Fali family of traders and government ministers, one of whom even had a Shi'ite invocation on his seal. The city's largest mosque was the Shi'ite Jalalabad mosque, and the monarchs sponsored the annual commemoration of the martyrdom of Imam al-Husayn, Shi'ism's main distinct commemoration. In 1387, under the rule of Tahamtan II's grandson, a minaret was added to the shrine of a religious scholar named Shaykh Rukn al-Din Danyal. It had both the names of the four rightly guided caliphs recognized by Sunnis and the twelve imams of the Shi'ites.

---

9 The inscriptions are cited from Alwazzan, "Politics," 153.

In terms of other shrines, when Ibn Battuta visited Hormuz, he reported a shrine of al-Khidr and Elijah six miles outside the city (Old Hormuz), known for its miracles, where there was also a lodge run by a Sufi shaykh who provided food to travellers. At one end of the island, there also lived a former merchant who after performing the pilgrimage to Mecca had taken up the life of an isolated holy man in a cave, but who also had cattle and sheep tended by slaves. He had entrusted his wealth to a brother, who now managed the business on his behalf. The Bibi Maryam mausoleum was also a pilgrimage site in modern times, and might have been for centuries, fulfilling the same spiritual functions as the sites associated with holy figures described in our opening chapter.

* * *

As this chapter has shown, the famous port of Hormuz epitomized many of the patterns of Persian Gulf history. These include an emphasis on commerce, ethnic and religious diversity, and a tradition of maritime knowledge. As with many other Gulf polities, it also maintained a *de facto* autonomy from mainland powers. And while it would continue into the 1600s under Portuguese domination, ultimately it would fade as have Siraf and Kish, replaced by nearby Bandar Abbas on the Iranian mainland.

Conclusion

The Portuguese came to power in the Gulf in part by exploiting the rivalries within the politics of Hormuz, particularly those between Arabs and Persians and kings and their viziers. They made Hormuz's ruler into their vassal, and then gradually took more and more direct control of Hormuz's government operations, though they seldom became involved further up the Gulf. Their presence reoriented the trade of some products towards Western Europe. The society and culture of the Gulf changed little, however, nor did most of the economic activity. The Gulf traders would even rally behind the Portuguese when their management of commercial life was seen as better than that of the Safavids, a dynasty which began ruling Iran at the same time.[1] In this way, despite this book ending at a conventional delineation of what is "medieval," that delineation is itself in many respects artificial.

The medieval history of the Gulf is important to the history of the medieval Middle East more generally. Particularly during the earlier centuries, its ports were among the largest cities in the region, a fact that is obscured by the fact they usually lasted for only short periods and so did not produce the sorts of texts produced for local pride that exist as pri-

---

1 The continuation of Gulf political patterns into Portuguese times is identified in Valeria Piacentini Fiorani, "The Gulf: A Cosmopolitan Mobile Society—Hormuz, 1475–1515 CE," in *The Gulf in World History*, ed. Fromherz, 35–55 at 51.

mary source material for other areas. Yet Baghdad, Aleppo, and other centres would not have the culture they did if not for the Gulf. Many goods traded through the Indian Ocean network came to play an important role in elite and even non-elite culture throughout the region. The web of people, places, and practices through which they entered the region matters to understanding the formation of the whole culture.

Furthermore, while the medieval Middle East in general is more diverse than generally recognized, the Gulf region stands out for its direct connections to multiple regions of non-Middle Eastern cultures with a regular population of people voyaging to them and maintaining their livelihoods by those connections. The Gulf was a region of interconnection and mobility, seen archaeologically in the distribution of artifacts and historically in the movement of trading communities to new settlements when conditions merited. Although the landed empires occasionally sought to control it, the region consistently reasserted its autonomy. The Seljuq Qavurd Khan established authority by making the Gulf of Oman the centre of his domains, prefiguring Hormuz.

The history of the medieval Persian Gulf also matters for the Gulf region today. The Gulf often appears to be a region without history, an impression which this book contributes to putting to rest. In addition, much of the substance of that history from the centuries covered in this book adds context to understanding the present. The political culture of competitive independent ports, for example, illuminates the existence of the small Arab Gulf states from an angle other than British intervention. The ethnic diversity found today in the oil-rich Arabian Peninsula states and Iran's ports is also part of a long historical pattern, as is the influence of diverse cultures. At the same time, religious tension between Sunnis and Shi'ites, while it has happened before, is not inevitable. The fact historical claims are often part of the debates among modern national and religious group necessitates familiarity with the history in order to evaluate such claims and place them in context.

Beyond the Middle East, the Gulf history is also relevant to the history of the Indian Ocean region. The medieval Indian Ocean's many branches are beset by a lack of written records. Like the Red Sea, the Persian Gulf is an exception, and so serves as an illustration of the sort of littoral society that existed across large stretches of the ocean's shores. From the standpoint of the Indian Ocean, it is noteworthy that the most important medieval shipwreck we have discovered was of a ship constructed in the Gulf, that Islam spread in trade entrepots throughout the basin, and Middle Eastern languages were used as languages of commerce.

Naturally, this book is only an overview of what we know at present, and far more research is underway. For too long, the Persian Gulf has represented a lacuna in people's historical sense of the Middle East and Islamic world, while the importance of earlier centuries for illuminating the present has been underappreciated. How might the distinct culture and environment of the Gulf have shaped the material culture of the medieval Middle East? How does earlier ports' acknowledgment of the overlordship of larger powers while maintaining autonomy compare to eastern Arabian ports' relationship with the British in more recent times? What distinctive features might the region's have in comparison with, say, the Malabar coast of India? These are just some of the larger questions more knowledge of this time and place can help us explore.

Further Reading

Agius, Dionisius. *Classic Ships of Islam: From Mesopotamia to the Indian Ocean*. Leiden: Brill, 2008.

> A detailed look and ships, ports, and seafaring in the medieval Middle East in both the Indian Ocean and Mediterranean Sea.

Alwazzan, Faisal Adel Ahmad. "Politics, Economy, and Religion in a Near Eastern Periphery: Baḥrayn in East Arabia *c*. 1050–*c*. 1400 CE." Ph.D. dissertation. University of Edinburgh, 2015. https://era.ed.ac.uk/handle/1842/31021.

> Indispensable pioneering study of the political, religious, and cultural history of eastern Saudi Arabia and Bahrain for the years indicated.

Aubin, Jean. "Le royaume d'Ormuz au début du XVIᵉ siècle." *Mare Luso-Indicum* 2 (1973): 77–179.

> An overview of Hormuz and its dependencies at the time of the Portuguese arrival

Averbuch, Bryan. "From Siraf to Sumatra: Seafaring and Spices in the Islamicate Indo-Pacific, Ninth–Eleventh Centuries C.E." PhD diss., Harvard University, 2013.

> A highly accessible dissertation focused on Indian Ocean luxury goods from their origins through use in medieval Middle Eastern cities, including descriptions of Siraf and Sohar.

Carter, Robert. *Sea of Pearls: Seven Thousand Years of the Industry that Shaped the Gulf.* London: Arabian Publishing, 2012.

> An account of Persian Gulf pearling from ancient times to the present based on archaeology and sources in Western languages.

Chong, Alan and Stephen Murphy, eds. *The Tang Shipwreck: Art and Exchange in the 9th Century.* Singapore: Asian Civilisations Museum, 2017.

> A well-illustrated museum publication which includes the most up-to-date studies of the Belitung shipwreck.

Fromherz, Allen James, ed. *The Gulf in World History: Arabia at the Global Crossroads.* Edinburgh: Edinburgh University Press, 2018.

> A collection of essays on Gulf globalization primarily in the medieval and early modern periods.

George, Alain. "Direct Sea Trade Between Early Islamic Iraq and Tang China: From the Exchange of Goods to the Transmission of Ideas." *Journal of the Royal Asiatic Society* 25 (2015): 579–624.

> An excellent overview of early Islamic trade through the Persian Gulf with China, including its cultural impact.

al-Ghunaym, ʿAbd Allāh Yūsuf. *Kitāb al-luʾluʾ*, 2nd ed. Kuwait City: A. Y. al-Ghunaym, 1998.

> A mainly medieval account of pearling by a historian whose father was himself a pearl diver.

Grant, Philip and Talha Ahsan. "Dr. Philip Grant on the Zanj Revolt, 869–883 CE: A Slave Uprising against the Caliphate." April 12, 2021. In *Abbasid History Podcast*. Podcast audio, 56:46. https://abbasidhistorypodcast.libsyn.com/ep026-26-dr-philip-grant-on-the-zanj-revolt-869-883ce-a-slave-uprising-against-the-caliphate.

> A discussion based on the current state of knowledge on the Zanj Revolt of 869–883.

Jalālī Azīziyān, Ḥasan. *Tārīkh-i Ābādān dar rūzgār-i Islāmī*. Mashhad: Bonyād-i Pazūhishāyi Islāmī, 1999.

> A compilation of information about medieval Abadan including theories of its origins, economic and natural geography, and certain famous aspects of the city.

al-Janbī, ʿAbd al-Khāliq b. ʿAbd al-Jalīl. *Buḥūth taʾrīkhiyya wa jughrāfiyya dhāta ʿalāqa bi-sharq shibh jazīra al-ʿarabiyya*. Beirut: Dar al-Mahaja, 2015.

> A book addressing multiple issues in the history of what is now eastern Saudi Arabia.

Jewel of Muscat Project. *Jewel of Muscat*. https://www.jewelofmuscat.tv. Lingua Franca Television. Last accessed January 19, 2023.

> The official web site documenting the project to build a medieval dhow replica and sail it from Oman to Singapore.

Kozah, Mario, Abdulrahim Abu-Husayn, Saif Shaheen al-Murikhi, and Haya Al Thani, eds. *An Anthology of Syriac Writers from Qatar in the Seventh Century*. Piscataway: Gorgias, 2015.

> A set of English translations of Syriac texts from Beth Qatraye, with some also presented in the original language.

Lambourn, Elizabeth. *Abraham's Luggage: A Social Life of Things in the Medieval Indian Ocean World*. Cambridge: Cambridge University Press, 2018.

> A fascinating study in which the author uses a surviving twelfth-century packing list to examine the material conditions of medieval Indian Ocean traders away from home, including ships and life on board during voyages.

Pearson, Michael. *The Indian Ocean*. Abingdon: Routledge, 2003.

> A highly accessible survey of Indian Ocean history from ancient times to the present.

Petrie, Cameron A., David Whitehouse, Donald Whitcomb, and T. J. Wilkinson. *Siraf: History, Topography and Environment*. Oxford: Oxbow, 2010.

Describes the environment, layout, and various buildings in Siraf based on twentieth-century excavations.

Piacentini Fiorani, Valeria. *Beyond Ibn Hawqal's Bahr al-Fārs: 10th–13th Centuries AD: Sindh and the Kīj-u-Makrān Region, Hinge of an International Network of Religious, Political, Institutional and Economic Affairs*. British Archaeological Reports, International Series 2651. Oxford: Archaeopress, 2014.

A study of the political economy in the indicated centuries of the Persian Gulf and Arabian Sea as far as the delta of the Indus River, including details on Buyid and Seljuq influence, Kish, and the rise of Hormuz.

Potter, Lawrence G., ed. *The Persian Gulf in History*. New York: Palgrave Macmillan, 2009.

An edited compilation of essays surveying the Persian Gulf from antiquity until the present.

Priestman, Seth M. N. *Ceramic Exchange and the Indian Ocean Economy (AD 400–1275)*. 2 vols. London: British Museum, 2021.

An analysis of the Indian Ocean's trade in ceramics during the indicated period, including details about the main sites with considered remains.

al-Ramhurmuzi, Buzurg b. Shahriyar. *The Book of the Marvels of India*. Translated by L. Marcel Devic and Peter Quennell. London: Routledge, 1928.

Although probably not by the author to whom it is attributed, this is still a premier collection of medieval Indian Ocean seafaring stories.

al-Salimi, Abdulrahman and Eric Staples, eds. *The Ports of Oman*. Hildesheim: Olm, 2017.

An edited compilations of essays on various Omani port cities from ancient times until the present.

Schine, Rachel and Ashher Masood. "Race and Islamic History with Dr. Rachel Schine." April 10, 2021. In *Bottled Petrichor*. Podcast audio, 51:33. https://www.youtube.com/watch?v=sndBMcXPvGg.

> A discussion of attitudes towards human blackness in the medieval Middle East.

Shafiq, Suhanna. *Seafarers of the Seven Seas: The Maritime Culture in the Kitāb ʿAjāʾib al-Hind (The Book of the Marvels of India) by Buzurg Ibn Shahriyār (d. 399/1009)*. Berlin: Schwarz, 2013.

> A study of the *Book of the Marvels of India* that culminates in an investigation of various seafaring terms found in the text.

Sheriff, Abdul. *Dhow Cultures of the Indian Ocean: Cosmopolitanism, Commerce and Islam*. London: Hurst, 2010.

> A historical overview of the littoral societies of the western Indian Ocean.

Sirry, Mun'im. *Controversies over Islamic Origins: An Introduction to Traditionalism and Revisionism*. Newcastle-upon-Tyne: Cambridge Scholars, 2021.

> An overview of the various historiographic controversies surrounding Islamic origins.

Soucek, Svat. *The Persian Gulf: Its Past and Present*. Costa Mesa: Mazda, 2008.

> A survey of Persian Gulf history from ancient times to the present.

Steve, Marie-Joseph. *L'île de Khārg, une page de l'histoire du Golfe Persique et du monachisme oriental*. In collaboration with Claire Hardy-Gilbert, Christelle and Florence Jullien, and Erik Smekens, and contributions from Farrokh Gaffary, Ernie Haernick, Emile Puech, and Axelle Rougeulle. Neuchatel: Recherches et Publications, 2003.

> The most important archaeological publication for Kharg Island.

Wilkinson, John. C. *Ibâḍism: Origins and Early Development in Oman*. Cambridge: Cambridge University Press, 2010.

A study of the development and spread of Ibadism that pays close attention to its social and political contexts.

Printed and bound by CPI Group (UK) Ltd, Croydon, CR0 4YY

27/03/2025

14649108-0001